PATRICIA HYNES, ANNA SKEELS AND
LAURA DURÁN

WITH A FOREWORD BY
ELEANOR LYONS

HUMAN TRAFFICKING OF CHILDREN AND YOUNG PEOPLE

A Framework for Creating Stable and
Positive Futures

First published in Great Britain in 2025 by

Policy Press, an imprint of
Bristol University Press
University of Bristol
1–9 Old Park Hill
Bristol
BS2 8BB
UK
t: +44 (0)117 374 6645
e: bup-info@bristol.ac.uk

Details of international sales and distribution partners are available at
policy.bristoluniversitypress.co.uk

© Patricia Hynes, Anna Skeels and Laura Durán, 2025

The digital PDF and ePub versions of this title are available open access and distributed under the terms of the Creative Commons Attribution-NonCommercial-NoDerivatives 4.0 International licence (https://creativecommons.org/licenses/by-nc-nd/4.0/) which permits reproduction and distribution for non-commercial use without further permission provided the original work is attributed.

British Library Cataloguing in Publication Data
A catalogue record for this book is available from the British Library

ISBN 978-1-4473-7501-2 paperback
ISBN 978-1-4473-7502-9 ePub
ISBN 978-1-4473-7503-6 ePdf

The right of Patricia Hynes, Anna Skeels and Laura Durán to be identified as authors of this work has been asserted by them in accordance with the Copyright, Designs and Patents Act 1988.

All rights reserved: no part of this publication may be reproduced, stored in a retrieval system, or transmitted in any form or by any means, electronic, mechanical, photocopying, recording, or otherwise without the prior permission of Bristol University Press.

Every reasonable effort has been made to obtain permission to reproduce copyrighted material. If, however, anyone knows of an oversight, please contact the publisher.

The statements and opinions contained within this publication are solely those of the authors and not of the University of Bristol or Bristol University Press. The University of Bristol and Bristol University Press disclaim responsibility for any injury to persons or property resulting from any material published in this publication.

Bristol University Press and Policy Press work to counter discrimination on grounds of gender, race, disability, age and sexuality.

Cover design: Ruth Wallace
Front cover image: iStock/Filo

Contents

List of abbreviations		iv
Acknowledgements		v
Foreword by Eleanor Lyons		vii
one	Understanding the human trafficking of children and young people	1
two	Methods and ethics: a shared participatory approach	25
three	Non-discrimination in principle and practice	44
four	In whose best interests?	63
five	The search for safety and restoring everyday life	82
six	Child participation and agency	106
seven	Development and implementation of a Positive Outcomes Framework	123
eight	Conclusions, new insights and new directions from child-centred research	139
Notes		153
References		155
Index		170

List of abbreviations

CCE	child criminal exploitation
CSA	child sexual abuse
CSE	child sexual exploitation
CSF	Creating Stable Futures
CSF-POF	Creating Stable Futures Positive Outcomes Framework
CSF-PT	Creating Stable Futures Practice Tool
ECPAT	Every Child Protected Against Trafficking
ESOL	English for speakers of other languages
GCM	Global Compact for Safe, Orderly and Regular Migration
GCR	Global Compact on Refugees
GP	general practitioner
ICTA	Independent Child Trafficking Advocate
ICTG	Independent Child Trafficking Guardianship
MSA 2015	Modern Slavery Act 2015
MSCOS	Modern Slavery Core Outcome Set
NRM	National Referral Mechanism
SDGs	Sustainable Development Goals (UN)
SEND	special educational needs and disabilities
UASC	unaccompanied asylum-seeking child
UNCRC	United Nations Convention on the Rights of the Child
YPAG	Young People's Advisory Group

Acknowledgements

Most importantly, our thanks and acknowledgement go to the young people across Scotland, Wales and England who took part in both research studies included in this book. Without their participation, and the organisations and practitioners who supported them, this book could not have been written. Special thanks go to BACA and Aberlour Scottish Guardianship Service for their support during this project.

Thanks and acknowledgements also go to ECPAT UK and the broader research team members of the initial Creating Stable Futures study – Patricia Durr, Elias Matar and Helen Connolly – whose commitment to ensuring safe spaces in which young people could speak and participate freely was indispensable and essential. We also give our gratitude and acknowledgments to the broader team members of the subsequent follow-on project – Maja Robaszkiewicz and Imogen Spencer-Chapman – both a vital source of ideas and solutions and both untiring and determined to utilise the Creating Stable Futures Positive Outcomes Framework (CSF-POF), develop the Creating Stable Futures Practice Tool (CSF-PT), and then engage with hundreds of frontline practitioners and professionals across Scotland, Wales, Northern Ireland and England to hear their feedback on both tools.

Throughout, many other colleagues have supported us. Within the Helena Kennedy Centre for International Justice, both Sital Dhillon and James Banks have believed in this project from the outset and supported the production of this book in many ways. Within Sheffield Hallam University, Jane Amner, Andrea Berg, Loretta Chantry-Groves, Emma Griffiths, Sarah Johnson-Mitchell, Tanya Miles-Berry, Craig Paterson, Sarah Pearson, Pete Smith, Clare Tudor, Bea Turpin and Samm Wharam, among others, have also been a continuous source of support. We also thank and acknowledge Rachel Witkin and Arnas Tamasauskas from the Helen Bamber Foundation for the work we did together on the divide between child and adult services and how this might be bridged though a focus on outcomes.

For the Modern Slavery Outcomes study, many thanks are due to Rebecca Griffiths, Emma Hawley, and Allyson Davies from the Barnardo's Independent Child Trafficking Guardianship (ICTG) service for their practice-focused steer and support for the participation of both ICTG service practitioners and young people in the research. This research has involved a co-designed approach, enabling deep understanding of the ICTG service. Such collaboration is essential for achieving a balance where the research is safe, relevant and appropriate for children as well as of quality, independent and robust. Thanks and acknowledgements also go to Dr Julia Thomas, external technical adviser on Q-methodology, and Hannah Stott from Safe to Grow for her child modern slavery expertise.

Projects like this do not happen without creative funders and our thanks go to the Modern Slavery and Human Rights Policy and Evidence Centre (MSPEC) for the original Creating Stable Futures and Modern Slavery Outcomes research funding and the Arts and Humanities Research Council (AHRC) for the original and follow-up Creating Stable Futures and Modern Slavery Outcomes funding. The team at Policy Press have also been incredibly helpful throughout, including Isobel Bainton, Rupert Spurrier and Rich Kemp. Thanks also to the helpful peer review comments which enriched this manuscript and to Helen Flitton for the project management and precise proofing involved.

Finally, to our families, Mark, Rob, Jack, Nolan, Emilio and Ciarán, who have enabled the space for this work to be completed, we are grateful.

Foreword

Eleanor Lyons
Independent Anti-Slavery Commissioner

Child trafficking is a heinous violation of the most basic of human rights – the right to have a childhood. Children can be trafficked by criminals for child sexual exploitation, criminal activities, forced marriage, labour exploitation, and/or domestic servitude. It can be hard for children to understand what is happening to them, particularly if they have been groomed by criminals, but the physical and psychological trauma endured often reverberates throughout their lives. Such exploitation is child abuse, and it can happen to any child. Its scars run deep. Without a clear, strategic and measurable path to recovery, these children remain vulnerable to further harm and revictimisation.

Preventing exploitation and protecting child victims is a priority area of my strategic plan as Independent Anti-Slavery Commissioner. I have heard from survivors about their exploitation, which started as a child and may have been prevented had there been more understanding of the types and risks of exploitation and more focused interventions from a young age. Overall, there is a lack of data about the experiences of children affected by trafficking, particularly from child victims themselves. This has been a barrier to addressing their needs, particularly how best to provide these interventions and, most importantly, deliver trauma-informed care.

This book offers a critical insight of the systems currently in place and ideas about how these can be improved for a better way forward. What is more, it is derived from the perspectives of children themselves and their experiences. This is our most valuable resource in shaping effective policies and interventions. By better understanding and defining what child trafficking means for children, we can ensure that every intervention – from medical care and psychological support to education and legal justice – is designed with the child's overall wellbeing, recovery and future in mind. A systematic multi-agency approach would allow us to track progress, adjust strategies as needed, and hold ourselves accountable for the promises made to these vulnerable children.

As this book sets out, there is more work to be done to ensure that definitions and terminology connected with child trafficking are accurate and clear so they can be effectively operationalised by professionals in the support of children wherever they are in the UK. This is why I co-commissioned a piece of work with the Modern Slavery Policy and Evidence Centre (MSPEC), delivered by Every Child Protected Against Trafficking (ECPAT UK), that seeks to address challenges posed by a lack of consensus among decision-makers and practitioners, around child trafficking. The work aims to shed more light on how practitioners currently understand differences in terms and promote the consensus needed to enable a consistent and effective response to child trafficking.

As this book rightly states 'definitions hold power', and they can have a significant impact on not just a child's immediate recovery but also on long-term outcomes. Children affected by trafficking are traumatised, then often thrust into a complex and sometimes retraumatising journey throughout their young lives, with little understanding of what is involved and what their future will hold. Vulnerability and trauma do not end at turning 18. Child victims of modern slavery need to be supported throughout their childhood and their transition to adulthood. As this book highlights, this is not only crucial in their recovery journey but in reducing the risk of retrafficking.

We have a real opportunity to radically reset how the system responds to a child affected by trafficking. This must be seen as the beginning of a new chapter and not as a 'job done'. The starting point must be listening to children and designing support around their needs. We must look to establish clear outcomes frameworks that are more than just sets of metrics, but are blueprints for change, setting clear, attainable goals that address not only immediate safety but also the long-term healing and empowerment that all children deserve.

ONE

Understanding the human trafficking of children and young people

Background and introduction

And it's really stressful, it makes young people sometimes stop what they're doing to achieve their dreams, all of that, so it's really difficult you know, the way the system is, especially I think ... if you don't have enough support. (2022)*

I don't have paper. Not free. Still in prison. (2022)

And we always have to start at the beginning. And after we tell the stories it brings back the memories and leaves us feeling bad again. (2022)

And these young people, they're going to be someone in the future and they're going to give back all that help they got from this government and it's very important

---

* All quotations from young people in this book are from the two studies contained herein unless stated otherwise. All names and locations have been anonymised.

for young people and support workers to know all of this. (2022)

OK, if I want to talk about being believed or ... my voice being heard ... the first when I came here, nobody listened to my story or – I refused and not believed. (2023)

We have recently seen the tenth anniversary of the introduction of the Modern Slavery Act 2015 (MSA 2015) in the UK. These words from children and young people** from England, Scotland and Wales have relevance to the implementation of this Act and are central to what this book is about. They begin to reveal some of the lived experiences of young people migrating to, and from within, the UK who have been affected by human trafficking, 'modern slavery',[†] diverse forms of exploitation, and associated abuse. They begin to capture the structural barriers these young people encounter during their active search for international protection, safety and the ability to move forward physically and emotionally with their lives.

This book is concerned with outcomes for these children and young people – in particular, positive outcomes identified both by and with them, during two participatory studies. The first of these studies is entitled Creating Stable Futures: Human Trafficking, Participation and Outcomes for Children (hereafter referred to as the 'CSF study' or 'first study'[††]). This was

---

[**] Article 1 of the UN Convention on the Rights of the Child defines a child as being under the age of 18 years. In this book the terms 'child', 'children' and 'young person' are used interchangeably, with the use of 'young person' intended to capture the 18–25 age range, which reflects care leaver entitlements up to age 21 or 25 if in higher education.

[†] The term 'modern slavery' has gained prominence due to the Modern Slavery Act 2015 but is contested, often presented in inverted commas as a result. For ease of reading, we have not used inverted commas throughout this book.

[††] All 2022 quotations cited in the book are from this study.

conducted between September 2021 and October 2022 with young people in England and Scotland, in partnership with Every Child Protected Against Trafficking (ECPAT UK). The second study, conducted between March 2023 and January 2024, was entitled Outcomes for Children and Young People Affected by Modern Slavery (hereafter referred to as the 'MS Outcomes study', the 'ICTG service study' or the 'second study'[§]); it analyses outcomes within the Independent Child Trafficking Guardianship (ICTG) service for England and Wales run by Barnardo's. This service is currently operational in two thirds of local authorities in England and Wales, pending its complete rollout in 2025–26, 10 years on from provision being made in the MSA 2015.

Both studies were focused on positive outcomes for these and other children and young people affected by human trafficking. Both studies used creative, participatory methods and followed similar approaches. Both were keenly concerned with the rights of the child, including rights to protection and participation and how these are enabled, supported and inherently interrelated. Combined, they focused on positive changes in practice to improve children and young people's lives.

These two studies valued the contributions of children and young people and their role in knowledge production and research. This involved drawing on young people's strengths and capabilities and on their endurance of complex and often protracted immigration, social care and criminal justice processes. Young people engaged shared their personal histories and original motivations for migration and how they found strength to navigate the many stresses they encountered. Neither study focused on raw accounts of exploitation or harm, but rather on understanding what positive outcomes could look like, as defined by children and young people themselves. Young people also described continuing to work

---

[§] All 2023 quotations cited in the book are from this study.

towards their aspirations and dreams despite encountering multiple barriers.

Little evidence is available on children and young people with lived experiences of human trafficking across the UK. What does exist, often within the grey literature, relates to awareness raising and lists of indicators around particular forms of exploitation and of children going missing, as well as policy mechanisms such as the National Referral Mechanism (NRM). This includes a focus on statistics and numbers of referrals into this identification mechanism (Kelly and Bokhari, 2012b; Rigby et al, 2012; Setter, 2017; ECPAT UK, 2019, 2022). There is room for further, deeper, richer and more nuanced discussion about how children and young people enter into and then exit exploitative contexts. Structural factors are rarely considered or elaborated, and the backstories of trafficking become invisible within a focus on UK exigencies.

This book, however, is uniquely and deliberately focused on the post-trafficking lives, looking directly at ways children and young people might achieve their human rights, as per the UK's obligations under international law. We propose how such progress could be assessed in practice, with specific goals set within an outcomes framework centred on their rights. In this way this book goes beyond ideas of 'rescue' of 'victims', as merely relating to a particular point of time and freedom from the people involved in their trafficking. Rather than a continued focus on the past, and what Grant has outlined as an over focus on 'exploitative experiences and immediate support needs' rather than 'narratives of recovery' (Grant, 2023: 9), this book provides a framework by which a child or young person's multi-faceted progress towards a happy, healthy life can be viewed. This framework, devised with young people, provides a way of seeing their rights that is unrestricted and non-prescriptive. Words spoken by young people throughout also provide sensitively and rarely accumulated evidence essential for policy and practice in this area.

We are not alone in making a case for a more positive focus on post-migration or post-trafficking outcomes. As Chase and Allsopp (2021) outline, 'life projects', and 'the stuff of dreams', help us conceptualise youth migration in a more balanced way:

> Certainly, youth migration needs to be understood in relation to its negative drivers of persecution, violence and unsustainable lives in countries of origin, factors that motivated the flights of many young people in this research. But at the same time, there is a need to recognize that such adversity also fuels individual and collective dreams and aspirations for better lives. (2021: 2)

The focus of this book is on how to think about such dreams and aspirations practically, through a discussion of desired positive outcomes as detailed by young people. It is well known that human trafficking involves human rights abuses and violations resulting in a whole host of negative health and other consequences (Ottisova et al, 2016; Cannon et al, 2017; Ibrahim et al, 2019). Without over-romanticising young people's abilities to overcome such barriers and trauma, the positive outcomes detailed herein emerged out of workshops with young people where the desire to actively build their presents and futures was a main preoccupation. More broadly, research into migration is increasingly focusing on aspirations and desires (Carling, 2014; Carling and Collins, 2018). This book is also concerned with professionals' responses to young people affected by human trafficking and the messages young people had for those professionals.

To aid understanding and provide background on the human trafficking of children and young people, this chapter will first consider international protections for children and then the international definition of human trafficking and its distinction from human smuggling. The UK context and existing child protection system will then be considered in respect of human trafficking and a more recent focus on modern slavery. We will reflect on what all of this means for the aspirations of and outcomes for children and young people affected by human trafficking. This chapter concludes with the aims of this book and a more detailed outline of subsequent chapters.

International protections for children

Globally, protection and support for children and young people who have experienced human trafficking or other forms of child abuse are particularly challenging areas of work (Pinheiro, 2006; Radford et al, 2011; Radford et al, 2015a,b; Guedes et al, 2016a,b; Radford et al, 2020; Jewkes et al, 2021; Maternowska et al, 2021, 2024). There is scant evidence available on 'what works' in child protection (Radford, 2017) and much less evidence that relates to child protection or safeguarding of children and young people affected by human trafficking.

There is also no single current piece of legislation that systematically addresses the lives of children amid migration (Bhabha and Dottridge, 2016). However, the multiple risks to the protection of these children amid displacement have been outlined (Boyden and Hart, 2007), with older children especially 'at risk of trafficking, armed recruitment, gender-based violence, abduction, exploitation and rape' (Kastberg, 2002: 4). Such displacement disrupts or removes the often-protective factors of education, family, friends or other critical social support networks contributing to these children's safety. Too often, international protection fails to be informed by the reality of children's lives or to address their specific protection needs.

As Bhabha (2009) suggests, Hannah Arendt has questioned who has the 'right to have rights', which relates closely to children who migrate. For Bhabha these are 'Arendt's children', functionally stateless, their theoretical rights under international law rarely enforced in practice (see also Meloni and Humphris, 2021). Bhabha (2016) has also highlighted how children who are trafficked or smuggled tend to fall under criminalising rather than protective approaches under international trafficking law, which does not require states to treat victims of trafficking with the same long-term protection as for refugees. There remains a need to strengthen effective access to protection by resourcing child protection services and integrating the protection of all those separated or unaccompanied as a matter of urgency, including but not exclusively for children and young people affected by human trafficking.

Internationally, the 1989 United Nations Convention on the Rights of the Child (UNCRC) provides a comprehensive framework for international legal standards for the protection and development of all children, offering such a protective rather than criminalising approach. In addition, the nature of children's rights as defined in the UNCRC – as universal, inalienable and indivisible – enables a holistic perspective on children who have lived experience of human trafficking. This is counter to the partial view often accompanying their criminalisation and essential for any appropriate consideration of outcomes for them and their lives (Bhabha and Dottridge, 2017).

The UNCRC is the most widely ratified human rights treaty internationally, including by the United Kingdom. Within its 54 Articles, it sets out the human rights of children, with four of these widely considered as 'General Principles'. Article 2 on non-discrimination seeks to ensure that all children have the same rights, without discrimination of any kind. Article 3 outlines how the 'best interests' of children should be a primary consideration in all actions concerning them. Article 6 recognises that every child has the inherent right to life and that State Parties have positive obligations to ensure survival and development. Article 12 articulates children's right to participation wherein children are considered capable of forming their own views and have the right to express those views freely and, crucially, as authors such as Lundy (2007) have suggested, have them heard. These four General Principles underpin how the Convention should be interpreted and put into practice. Each is explored further (see Chapters 3 to 6). Hanson and Lundy (2017) have suggested that these four principles are often used as an 'accessible shorthand for the child rights project as a whole' (2017: 288) but are interdependent and overlap with other Articles in the UNCRC.

This focus on children's participation, in addition to their protection, is key. Protection can confer vulnerability and dependency on the part of the child, whereas participation invokes capabilities, capacity and agency (Sen, 1999). This tension is an important perspective to hold onto if we are to consider all the potential outcomes for children and young people affected by modern slavery and fully reflect their 'human potential and how this can and should be respected and represented' (Maguire in Carter, 2009: 861).

In addition, and of particular relevance here, the Convention is also concerned with the distinct needs and protection rights of children temporarily or permanently separated from their family environment (Article 20) and children suffering exploitation (Article 19). These include effective procedures for the establishment of social programmes to provide necessary support for the child as well as for other forms of prevention, treatment and follow-up for these forms of abuse.

According to Howard and Okyere, the broad ratification of the UNCRC, has 'inspired major global consciousness on the state of childhood and children's rights' (2022: 2) and underpins dominant discourses in international child protection. However, child rights violations remain commonplace worldwide, including the inhumane ways child refugees and asylum-seekers are treated in some countries. An example from the UK could be the gulf between children's rights under international law and young people finding themselves in detention due to inaccurate age assessments or instances of their being denied family reunification rights. There is a substantial gap, then, between the promises of the Convention and the reality of many children's lives. In addressing this gap between the way international law is perceived and enforced in practice, Howard and Okyere argue a need for researchers and practitioners to become more political and participatory: 'no matter how well intentioned we are, we are unlikely to be able to understand the nuances of another's circumstances sufficiently well to be able to build appropriate interventions without them. ... The avoidance of harm therefore requires us to adopt more participatory approaches' (2022: 221–2). Main critiques of the UNCRC, like other laws that purport universality, include how it enshrines Western notions of 'childhood' and Eurocentric modes of thought. This exclusion of the legacies of colonialism and imperialism provides an inadequate representation of the diversity of the world's children and 'childhoods' (Hart, 2006; Faulkner and Nyamutata, 2020). Other critiques are raised throughout this book (Anderson, 2012; O'Connell Davidson, 2013; Hanson and Lundy, 2017; Howard and Okyere, 2022; Stalford and Lundy, 2022).

What is human trafficking?

Human trafficking and human smuggling are not new phenomena, finding prominence in the past two decades on both global and national policy agendas as major social issues of global concern (Morrison and Crosland, 2001; Gallagher, 2015b; Zimmerman et al, 2015; Kiss and Zimmerman, 2019). At a global governance level, human trafficking features in both the Global Compact on Refugees (GCR) and the Global Compact for Safe, Orderly and Regular Migration (GCM),[1] with forced displacement often considered to increase risks of trafficking or exploitation en route and within destination countries. Global initiatives such as the UN Sustainable Development Goals (SDGs) and their targets additionally detail human trafficking, exploitation, modern slavery, and the worst forms of child labour in Goals 5, 8, 10 and 16. For example, Target 8.7 specifically focuses on effective measures to eradicate forced labour, modern slavery and human trafficking as well as the worst forms of child labour.

A landmark definition of human trafficking was provided in 2000 in a supplementary Protocol[2] to the Convention against Transnational Organized Crime (hereafter referred to as 'the Palermo Protocol') (Gallagher, 2015a). Article 3(a) provided an internationally accepted definition of 'trafficking in persons' to mean:

> ... the recruitment, transportation, transfer, harbouring or receipt of persons, by means of the threat or use of force or other forms of coercion, of abduction, of fraud, of deception, of the abuse of power or of a position of vulnerability or of the giving or receiving of payments or benefits to achieve the consent of a person having control over another person, for the purpose of exploitation. Exploitation shall include, at a minimum, the exploitation of the prostitution of others or other forms of sexual exploitation, forced labour or services, slavery or practices similar to slavery, servitude or the removal of organs.

This definition, with its three parts – the 'act', 'means' and 'purpose' – of human trafficking has been implemented globally. The 'act' of trafficking – the way it is carried out – is in the recruitment, transportation, transfer, harbouring or receipt of persons. The 'means' – how it is done – relates to threats involved or the giving or receiving payments or benefits. The reasons why trafficking takes place – the 'purpose' – includes sexual exploitation, forced labour, slavery, or practices similar to slavery and servitude. Only the 'act' and 'purpose' are necessary for a child under 18 years to be considered as a case of 'trafficking in persons', with the 'means' part irrelevant. This is not to say that this stage does not occur for child victims, but the definition recognises that a child can never consent to their own exploitation, even if he or she agrees or understands what has happened.

There is often confusion about the differences between human trafficking and human smuggling, with the two commonly used interchangeably. This can be partly due to similarities between them. For example, both are punishable offences, may involve transnational organised criminal groups and involve movement of people from one place to another. While human trafficking inherently involves exploitation, smuggling does not, though people on the move can become vulnerable to trafficking during or after the smuggling process (van Liempt, 2007). Other differences include that human trafficking can happen within a country and across international borders, whereas human smuggling always involves the crossing of an international border. People may be trafficked into a country through what are now termed 'regular routes' such as with a visa, but human smuggling involves moving people across a border now termed 'irregularly'. If someone is trafficked, they are considered a 'victim' of crime, whereas smuggling is an immigration offence against the state.

Definitions such as these then hold power and have implications for people's protection. The description of being 'smuggled' means different treatment to being 'trafficked'. The criminalising rather than protective approach of the Palermo Protocol can lead to people being punished or deported. Such 'removal' and 'rescue' from exploitation can lead to other unintended consequences that are not child-centred.

The UK child protection landscape

Within the UK, an established child protection system exists with a multi-agency framework devised to address child abuse and child maltreatment. Key child protection legislation is contained within the 1989 Children Act and, following Lord Laming's inquiry into the murder of Victoria Climbié, a subsequent 2004 Children Act. Child protection in the UK, as defined by UK government guidance, relates to four different types of child abuse: physical abuse, emotional abuse, sexual abuse, and neglect. The most comprehensive survey in the UK found that child maltreatment remains an experience for a substantial minority (25.3 per cent of all children) across physical assault, contact and non-contact sexual abuse, emotional abuse and neglect (Radford et al, 2011). This included abuse in the home, in school, in the community from adults and from peers.

However, as Parton (2014) has detailed, the numbers of referrals into children's social care more generally does not give realistic data on the prevalence and nature of child maltreatment experienced by children and young people. In other words, only a small proportion of child abuse becomes known to official agencies despite longstanding messaging and campaigns around child abuse being 'everybody's business'.

Much of the content of this book is relevant to safeguarding questions as a whole (Dixon et al, 2017). In recent years there have been steps forward in understanding and responding to human trafficking. In parallel, there have also been positive shifts in understanding child sexual exploitation (CSE) (Melrose and Pearce, 2013; Beckett et al, 2017; Hallet, 2017; Scott et al, 2019) and emergent knowledge about child criminal exploitation (CCE) (Barlow et al, 2021; Lloyd et al, 2023), both relating mainly to domestically born children. These worlds are now coming together with human trafficking under the NRM, with referrals from both UK- and non-UK-born children increasing year-on-year.

There has also been a welcome shift towards a contextual safeguarding approach in response to UK-born young people facing risk and/or extra-familial harm outside the family home (Firmin, 2020; Wroe and Manister, 2024). This approach, which shifts a longstanding stance of child protection being solely focused on younger children and abuses within the home, holds potential for children affected by exploitation, human trafficking or modern slavery in the way it considers risks outside family environments, detailing how risks and harms may be extra-familial (Huegler, 2021) as well as intra-familial.

'Transitional safeguarding' is another promising approach in terms of its use in practice for human trafficking. This approach, which outlines necessary shifts to create conditions for addressing risk and harms during a young person's transition to 'adulthood', highlights how safeguarding concerns for young people under 18 years are different for those over 18 years but also how experiences of risk and harm 'do not follow binarised notions of childhood and adulthood, often continuing beyond their 18th birthday' (Huegler, 2021). A key point is that this transition occurs at the same time as gaps in provision between child and adult services are recognised (see also Chase and Allsopp, 2021 and Chase, 2020). Holmes (2022) has outlined how a transitional safeguarding approach requires multi-agency, whole-systems change to reframe safeguarding from being service-centric, thresholds-based and shifting towards collaborative work *with*, rather than *on* or *for*, young people and their communities.

Relevant legislation, policy and practice mechanisms in the UK

Current UK legal, policy and practice frameworks about migration, refugee status, asylum, and human trafficking have been built up around multiple, and at times, competing discourses that are rarely neutral and are often political in nature (O'Connell Davidson, 2011). Over the past three decades, legislation and policies around detention, deportation, destitution, and the compulsory dispersal of those seeking sanctuary from persecution have been key policy tools, intended to deter people from entering the UK (Broad and Turnbull, 2019; Clayton et al, 2021; Hodkinson et al, 2021; Hynes, 2009, 2022). Simultaneously, there has been an introduction to human trafficking in public discourse and policy with a shift towards use of the term modern slavery following introduction of the MSA 2015 and equivalent legislation in other devolved administrations. Awareness about human trafficking and, since the introduction of the Act, modern slavery has grown significantly over the past decade.

Children's experiences of care, support and protection are shaped by these competing and shifting discourses that sit within complex immigration, criminal justice and social care processes rather than being shaped by children's needs, the realities of their experiences or, significantly, their own views. Such discourses position children in different ways and have real-world implications for them and their lives.

Children and young people who arrive into the UK can experience a different legislative, policy and practice universe to UK-born children and young people, with additional layers of complexity relating to their legal status, a tension between their welfare and immigration legislation, and increasingly fractioned protection mechanisms available (Zetter, 2007; Finch, 2014; Allsopp and Chase, 2019; Chase, 2020; Chase and Allsopp, 2021). Chase (2020), for example, details different legal outcomes for unaccompanied young people which are time-limited and discretionary periods of leave to remain until they become an adult. These are refugee status, time-limited 'unaccompanied asylum-seeking child' (UASC) leave (which requires further legal assistance upon approaching 17.5 years of age), refusal, humanitarian or discretionary leave. As such, tensions between care and control and the way young people arriving into the UK may have faced risks and/or extra-familial harm, not only outside the family home but also across different locations during their journeys to the UK, all require consideration. These other sets of risk and/or experiences of abuse or exploitation currently sit outside national frames of reference for child abuse.

As of the end of 2023, 17,004 people had been referred during that year into the UK's NRM[3] for identifying trafficking and providing associated support. Of these, 44 per cent were those who had been potentially exploited as children (n=7,432) representing the highest annual referral numbers of children since the establishment of the NRM in 2009. These referrals now include multiple and complex forms of exploitation, such as 'sexual and criminal exploitation' and 'labour and domestic exploitation'. It is likely that, as with child abuse, there will be a gulf between the number of children being referred into this trafficking mechanism and the actual numbers involved.

The trafficking of children and young people from within the UK is increasingly evident in referrals into the NRM as knowledge on such internal trafficking grows. Whereas a decade ago the UK was predominantly considered as a destination country for international child trafficking, it is now also a source country, particularly for children being referred for domestically driven CSE and increasingly spotlighting CCE.

The UK's MSA 2015 was considered progressive and cutting edge by many in government and within civil society on gaining Royal Assent in 2015. It includes the offences of servitude, forced or compulsory labour, and human trafficking under the umbrella term of modern slavery. Independent commentators focused on how asylum and immigration legislation and policy often create the conditions in which human trafficking, modern slavery and/or exploitation can thrive (Hynes, 2009, 2022; O'Connell Davidson, 2011; Anderson, 2012, 2013). The timing of this Act came shortly after 'hostile environment' policies were enacted within the UK Home Office which, as Clayton et al (2021) suggest, aimed to make the UK a hostile place for unwanted migration, resulting in performative cruelty towards those arriving 'irregularly' into the UK.

Slavery, forced labour and human trafficking have different historical and legal antecedents and the ways they are merged under the MSA is subject to ongoing debate (Chuang, 2014; ILO, 2012; Allain, 2018; Dottridge, 2017; Faulkner, 2020). Both as a term and an Act, modern slavery is subject to ongoing discussion and critique. For example, O'Connell (2024) outlines how the term gives a 'shallow reading of the history of slavery' (2024: 54). Engaging with literature on decolonisation and, in particular Quijano's concept of the 'coloniality of power' (2000), O'Connell suggests it privileges a 'narrow vision centred on an individualized relationship between "slaveholder" and "slave"' rather than more structural forces (O'Connell, 2024: 56). The power of the term also lies in its ability to invoke emotional responses through emotionally charged language that draws on examples of extreme brutality, sometimes elevated as a *cause célèbre* (LeBaron et al, 2021). This 'catch-all' or umbrella term now also connotes a broad and ever-expanding range of exploitative practices, described as an 'exploitation creep' (Chuang, 2014). To date, unlike human trafficking, there remains no internationally agreed definition of modern slavery (Allain, 2018; Broad and Turnbull, 2019).

Outside the UK, previous research shows that practitioners and professionals in source countries adopting the recognised international definition of human trafficking – and its 'act', 'means' and 'purpose' components in the Palermo Protocol – had little recognition of this being modern slavery (Hynes et al, 2019). For example, in Nigeria, a country with a long history of slavery and colonial labour abuses, the term was highly problematic (see also O'Connell Davidson, 2013; Dottridge, 2017[4]; Faulkner, 2024).

Protection of children with lived experience of trafficking

There are a few studies that specifically consider the child protection or safeguarding of children and young people affected by human trafficking (Rigby, 2011; Rigby et al, 2012; Pearce et al, 2013; Rigby and Ishola, 2016; Cockbain and Olver, 2019; Keeling and Goosey, 2021). Children classed as 'unaccompanied minors' or 'unaccompanied asylum-seeking children' in the UK are also represented in the literature (Hek et al, 2012; Meloni and Humphris, 2021) and there is some crossover around children going 'missing' from care and human trafficking (Setter, 2017; ECPAT UK and Missing People, 2019, 2022; Sidebottom et al, 2020).

Human trafficking can involve all or some of the four forms of child abuse defined under UK guidance. Children and young people may experience abuse or exploitation in a range of settings outside their homes and across different locations in and beyond the UK. Numbers of referrals into children's social care and/or the NRM are unlikely to give realistic data on the prevalence and nature of exploitation experienced. It could well be that only a small proportion of the trafficking of children becomes known to official agencies despite awareness raising efforts.

While it has been recognised for over a decade that human trafficking is child abuse, policy and practice often fail to engage with this premise and a 'criminalising' as well as 'immigration-centred discourse' rather than a 'child-centred discourse' often prevails (Bovarnick, 2010: 80; Pearce et al, 2013).

At present, the voices of children affected by human trafficking and exploitation are missing from policy development and any focus on short, medium or longer term 'outcomes' for these children is absent from debate. To understand whether efforts to protect children and young people are working, there must be ways to ask children and young people themselves. At a global level, the 2015 State of the World's Children report posed the question: 'What do refugee children need?' in terms of their protection and responded: 'Ask them!' (Skeels in UNICEF, 2015). However, subsequent literature at both global and UK levels continue to highlight a lack of meaningful participation of forcibly displaced children in their own protection, including those affected by human trafficking. There is further work needed for this to happen. For example, in relation to international child protection, Howard and Okyere suggest that 'the increased emphasis in research on children and young people's voices, lived experiences and participation has yet to impact policy and practice in substantial ways' (2022: iii).

Since the introduction of the MSA 2015 in the UK, there have been a series of legislative and policy developments relevant for children and young people including: a pilot of devolved NRM decision-making in ten local authorities across England, Scotland and Wales; a High Court ruling of 'unlawful' on the Home Office policy of accommodating unaccompanied children in hotels; and, the introduction of the 2022 Nationalities and Borders Act and the 2023 Illegal Migration Act, both adversely affecting progress made to date for identifying, supporting and protecting 'victims'/ 'survivors' of modern slavery. Local authorities retain the legal duty to safeguard children in their care regardless of their immigration status.

Introduction of Independent Child Trafficking Advocates/Guardians

Independent guardianship for all unaccompanied and separated children seeking asylum is a right that is embedded within international and European law and standards. Currently in England and Wales, this right is not available to all children and young people, other than those identified as being victims of modern slavery.

A particularly pertinent development for this book made possible under Section 48 of the MSA 2015 has been the establishment of provision for Independent Child Trafficking Advocates (ICTAs), now Guardians or ICTGs,[5] across England and Wales, to act in the best interests of children and young people under the age of 18.[6] Currently run by Barnardo's, the service reaches two thirds of local authorities across England and Wales and, as noted earlier, is in the process of being commissioned to cover both nations in full. This rollout has, however, been 'glacial' (Hynes, 2025) and staggered, with evaluations built-in at each step. While the value of ICTGs has become known through this series of Home Office evaluations (Kohli et al, 2015, 2019; Keeble et al, 2018; Shrimpton et al, 2020, 2024) plus the inclusion of a focus on ICTAs within an independent review of the Modern Slavery Act (Field et al, 2018), commissioned evaluations have not always substantively included children and young people's perspectives or what they feel have been the most important outcomes *for them*.

As such, any focus on 'outcomes' is not child-centred or child-informed. It mainly relates to the ways stakeholders in the UK's modern slavery, human trafficking and safeguarding sector refer to a child as having a 'reasonable grounds' or a 'conclusive grounds' outcome following referral into the NRM or specific legal outcomes as outlined earlier (Chase, 2020). Such procedural outcomes, while integral to formal identification and referral for support services as a victim of human trafficking, present a partial and limited perspective on the lived experience and recovery needs of children and young people affected by human trafficking.

What is meant by 'outcomes'?

Across international and national literature on human trafficking, there is considerable variance and inconsistencies on what is meant by the term 'outcome' (Hemmings et al, 2016; Ottisova et al, 2016; Batomen Kuimi et al, 2018; Cannon et al, 2018; Moynihan et al, 2018a,b; Simkhada et al, 2018; Dell et al, 2019; Graham et al, 2019; Ibrahim et al, 2019; Albright et al, 2020; Garg et al, 2020; Laird et al, 2020; Such et al, 2020; Malhorta and Elnakib, 2021; Knight et al, 2022). The international outcomes literature focuses mainly on specific health and healthcare outcomes studied through qualitative, mixed method and quantitative studies, prevalence and estimates of physical, sexual and mental health (Cannon et al, 2018; Ottisova et al, 2016; Batomen Kuimi et al, 2018; Simkhada et al, 2018; Ibrahim et al, 2019; Albright et al, 2020; Such et al, 2020). There is a lack of outcomes focus for other aspects of post-trafficking lives and only a few available systematic reviews beyond this medicalised focus (Cockbain et al, 2018; Okech et al, 2018; Dell et al, 2019; Knight et al, 2022).

There is also very limited evidence on the effectiveness of interventions, actual impacts or explicit theories of change that depict pathways to desired outcomes, and there are many unanswered questions around the measurement of outcomes (Bryant and Joudo, 2015; Forrester, 2017; Bryant and Landman, 2020). As Bryant and Landman (2020) suggest, anti-trafficking organisations focus on implementation and outputs rather than outcomes or impact. For example, a review by Dell et al (2019) considers exit and post-exit interventions for survivors of human trafficking, finding sparse evidence of the impact of interventions available and low quality, poorly designed studies that do not take into account the complexities and needs of trafficking survivors.

Measuring the impact of interventions is not straightforward. There is no single validated measure available for children affected by trafficking and any measurement would need to draw on a selection of existing standardised measures already utilised with children. Considerable work would be needed to consider which measures were appropriate and which relate to trafficking experiences. For children and young people affected by human trafficking, it is unlikely that available standardised measures or simple measurements alone could capture the complexities of their lives. However, there is already administrative data, social care, immigration, criminal justice, NRM, Looked After Children, Children in Need and child protection measurements that could contribute to such endeavours (Feinstein et al, 2021).

In the UK child protection and safeguarding worlds, outcomes relate to specific statements that professionals involved are looking to achieve through child protection plans. These tend to offer a final goal and are developed to address harms experienced and/or unmet needs. The outcomes are framed as specific, with associated actions and objectives in line with indicators to provide evidence towards final goals. In the CSF study, a definition of outcomes contained in a child-focused piece of work by the organisation What Works for Children's Social Care was utilised. This defined 'outcomes' as the consequences of an action, where an action is a particular service or way of working (La Valle et al, 2019).[7] The authors detail how the development of an outcomes' framework is a first step to improving local evidence and enabling well-informed decisions. This definition of 'outcomes' was also employed as a starting point in the MS Outcomes study. The focus on 'outcomes' in relation to the ICTG service as reporting requirements to the Home Office were explored. The ICTG service aims relate closely to outcome areas, including those about rights and service access, formal system navigation, building relationships and wellbeing and recovery, to holistically address the human trafficking of children and young people. Outcomes reported systematically by the ICTG service to the Home Office, however, present a more partial view, including, for example, type of exploitation and decision status relating to the NRM.

Aims and outline of this book

The human trafficking of children and young people is of considerable concern from a child rights and children's development perspective (Todres and Kilkelly, 2025). This book first aims to consider, and contribute to, the limited peer-reviewed literature and evidence base available on these children, where much of the output to date has been generated by the third sector. To do this, we draw on two studies and a range of sources, including national and international literature. Through this, we also seek to highlight and regenerate interest in and concern for this critical societal issue among duty bearers and decision-makers and to precipitate action.

This book further aims to detail and reflect on the research background, design and implementation of a newly conceptualised Creating Stable Futures Positive Outcomes Framework (CSF-POF), developed with and by young people affected by human trafficking and centred around Articles 2, 3, 6 and 12 of the UNCRC. These four General Principles were used to provide a human rights-based structure for the CSF-POF. Throughout we also report on the first-ever use of the CSF-POF as an evaluation tool in the MS Outcomes study in engaging young people to share their views and experiences on outcomes from Barnardo's ICTG service support.

These two aims combined allow us to make a significant contribution to academic, policy and practice debates on outcomes for children and young people affected by human trafficking in the UK. We champion the protection rights of children and young people, their potential to achieve positive outcomes across all areas of their lives and to have policy impact through their participation. In turn, we reposition children and young people affected by human trafficking and change the narrative on outcomes by utilising findings from our two studies.

Finally, this book repositions children affected by human trafficking and exploitation in relation to child protection and safeguarding in the UK and helps shift narratives on outcomes from legalistic, procedural outcomes to outcomes devised by young people themselves. The UK's child protection and safeguarding systems tend to focus on younger children and interventions within the family home. This model does not fit well with protection and safeguarding challenges around young people who have lived experience of exploitation and where there is extra-familial risk and harm. We therefore consider what a 21st century model of child protection and safeguarding for these young people involves in practice, including how this means accepting and understanding both risk and protective factors beyond and within the UK.

A key idea developed throughout will be that the human trafficking of children and different forms of child exploitation should be seen first and foremost as child abuse rather than as an immigration or criminal justice concern. Reflecting on the existing four forms of child maltreatment devised with younger children inside the family home in mind, we suggest that young people affected by trafficking do not fit neatly in this paradigm. However, we also suggest that 'exploitation' – as yet undefined and under-developed in the UK – could also sit alongside these four existing forms. This purposeful reframing could entail a journey to understanding abuses experienced by a range of children and young people – young and older, inside and outside the home – plus, crucially, bring in risk and protective factors that are transnational in nature but highly appropriate to a better understanding of human trafficking.

Current knowledge of the exploitation of children and young people from the UK relates mainly to known and existing forms of CSE and CCE. Current knowledge for children from beyond the UK sees additional categories of exploitation as well as these two forms. For these children domestic servitude and/or labour exploitation are also reflected in NRM referrals. The common thread running through these forms of child maltreatment is exploitation. We call here for further conceptualisation and research on this question as to whether 'exploitation' could or should be seen as a fifth form of child maltreatment alongside neglect, physical, emotional, and sexual abuse, so that our 21st century model of child protection and safeguarding for these young people suits their experiences and needs.

Following on from this introductory chapter, Chapter 2 reflects on the methodology, shared approach and ethical considerations involved in the two research studies herein. Chapters 3 to 6 detail the four General Principles of the UNCRC separately and what young people said about them in the context of UK systems and processes. Each of these principles will be explored and will include a wealth of rich, qualitative accounts of the experiences and views of young people.

Chapter 7 details the development of the CSF-POF. It is the first time that children and young people have been part of the development of such a framework. Based on what they said in workshops, it is therefore also the first time we know what young people identify as outcomes that are important and meaningful to them. The framework identifies what young people would need to see for positive changes to happen in their lives and the lives of others, now and in the future. The first efforts at employing the CSF-POF with young people affected by human trafficking by the MS Outcomes study to assess outcomes from the support service they receive is also set out in this chapter. This exploration of possible post-trafficking positive outcomes is set within a service dedicated to the rights of children. It details the process and methods selected to activate the framework as a measurement tool, as well as the challenges and learning involved.

Our Conclusion (Chapter 8) considers the evolving landscape of terminology in this field as well as key insights generated from these child-centred research studies. It reflects on whether exploitation should be considered a fifth form of child abuse in the UK and then highlights a contemporary issue wherein children transitioning from child to adult services face ongoing challenges for their protection. This final chapter brings together the different threads developed in previous chapters plus a reflection of the implications of the two studies for policy, practice and research in the UK. We also reflect on how research, as a process of possibility, can help bring the views, knowledge and experiences of children and young people into the centre of policy making.

TWO

Methods and ethics: a shared participatory approach

Introduction

> When I look at positive outcomes, it's where a young person has got to a place where they genuinely believe that what they have to say matters, that they have the right to speak up, that what happened to them was abusive, it was wrong. ... It's where their self-worth has grown ... [they do not] blame themselves for abuse, with huge levels of shame ... and can instead recognize their own strengths and actually have aspirations. (Interview 138, key informant, UK, May 2018, Hynes et al, 2019)

The idea for a study on positive outcomes was originally inspired by these words from an experienced professional during previous research (Hynes, 2019). The Creating Stable Futures: Human Trafficking, Participation and Outcomes for Children study sought to both understand the possibility of positive outcomes as well as what they might look like in practice. This demanded a participatory approach in order for the views and words of young people to be central. The following year, this study and the CSF-POF it produced were used as the basis of a participatory assessment with young people from the Independent Child Trafficking Guardianship (ICTG) service for England and Wales. This subsequent study, exploring outcomes for young people from ICTG service support, involved an innovative use of a participatory 'Q-methodology'.

This chapter is concerned with the shared participatory approach adopted by these two studies. Bringing these two UK-based participatory studies with young people together has also involved reflection on their separate analysis and sequential timings. Combined, this has provided the opportunity to reflect on what 'listening' to children and young people means in practice, what 'meaningful' inclusion in research looks like, and how a child-centred, rights-based approach can be achieved that is non-blaming, non-stigmatising and that creates safe spaces for participation. This chapter details the respective aims, methods, interpretation of data, analysis and ethical issues involved. It is important to say that each stage of this process required ethical consideration, from design to dissemination of findings.

While this chapter relays key learning from both studies on the use of participatory research with young people affected by human trafficking and the ethical considerations of doing so, Chapter 6 considers children's right to participation more broadly, including the views and experiences of the young people participating in this research.

Dimensions of a shared approach: voice, participation and protection

Conducting research into human trafficking, modern slavery and/or the exploitation of children and young people is a complex, multi-faceted and sensitive pursuit, requiring a keen responsibility and accountability to those affected and engaged. It involves a range of decisions on research questions and research design, approaches, methods, data analysis and the interpretation of data.

The work on international and domestic participatory research by others has underpinned our respective approaches (Hart and Tyrer, 2006; Pinheiro 2006; Lundy, 2007, 2018, 2025; Hart, 2008; Skeels, 2014; Warrington, 2020; Ozer et al, 2024). A key preoccupation for both studies in this book has been to address the lack of children and young people's 'voice' or, more fully, their lack of participation. Broadly, the use of participatory or action research approaches builds on underlying assumptions that those closest to or who have direct experience of the topic being researched not only hold expert and valid knowledge but may also be best placed to undertake the diagnosis of a problem and the development of solutions (Bryman, 2012; Ozer et al, 2024). This allows researchers and members of other social settings to collaborate in research that is relevant and combines lived experiences with independent research. Ozer et al's explanation of the historical context of participatory action research with young people illustrates how this has been undertaken across a wide range of disciplines and across two broad streams, referred to as 'the Northern and Southern hemisphere traditions' (Ozer et al, 2024: 403). While the 'Northern' tradition has been primarily focused on enhancing organisational practices, the 'Southern' tradition 'has explicit roots in empowerment' having emanated from 'broader struggles for rights and power by socially and economically marginalised groups' as elaborated by Paulo Freire (Ozer et al, 2024: 403). This approach means inside, lived experiences are key, challenging more traditional positivist approaches that value distance and objectivity.

For Lundy (2007) and others, a focus on 'voice' alone when working with children is, in fact, 'not enough'. It diminishes Article 12 of the United Nations Convention on the Rights of the Child (UNCRC), which gives children the right to not only express views but have these given due weight in all matters affecting them. Lundy's (2018) model of child and youth participation moves beyond a notion of 'voice' and considers this right to participation as foundational to the realisation of other child rights. It also places both the quality and impact of participation at its centre. The model was based on findings that children and young people felt their views were not being listened to or given full consideration (Lundy, 2007, 2018). It presents four key concepts – space, voice, audience, and influence – and has been utilised internationally to understand children's participation. These four concepts are interrelated and provide a model for rights-compliant participation of children and young people with:

- 'space', relating to the way children must be given opportunities to express their views through the creation of inclusive safe spaces;
- 'voice', ensuring that ways are found to ensure children are able to express their views;
- 'audience', relating to how these views need to be listened to; and
- 'influence', ensuring these views are acted upon and given due weight according to their age and maturity.

Pinheiro's (2006) first worldwide study of violence towards children – the *World Report on Violence against Children* – was a key moment in efforts both to address violence against children and for its involvement of children. The comprehensive involvement of children was itself a landmark in the development of participatory research on protection with children. Similarly, in research with children in situations of armed conflict and emergency contexts, Hart and Tyrer (2006) suggest that research should explore the lives of children from their own perspectives. They outline a rationale for child-centred research that recognises the agency, resilience and resourcefulness of children in the face of extreme adversity. Hart (2008) also suggests that participatory projects seeking to achieve the transformation of children's lives often pay little attention to the political contexts in which such transformation is sought. Such limitations of the approach focus on power, societal change and any necessary political will to achieve any transformation. Critiquing local participatory efforts that are disconnected to larger systems and structures of power, Hart suggests the use of socio-ecological models that nest children within concentric circles – from the individual, family, community, and often societal relationships – needs to also consider situational and contextual aspects if they are to provide insights into 'more systemic changes that would positively affect the lives of all' (Hart, 2008: 416). Moreover, Hart's work leaves open the possibility that forced migration may well have negative impacts, but simultaneously may also allow forced migrants opportunities and potential for reconfiguring their lives (Hart, 2014).

More recently, Warrington (2020) has suggested that young people with experiences of sexual violence gain 'protection through participation' by taking part in participatory work which increases the chances for their perspectives to be heard and considered by others. Warrington's work on key principles for promoting safe and empowering spaces for young people with experiences of sexual violence informed the Creating Stable Futures study. Warrington's suggestions relating to the UK resonate deeply with international research on refugee children's participation in protection (Skeels, 2014). As Skeels outlines: 'it indicates that there might be a relationship between child participation and protection – the suggestion being that if refugee children are capacitated to talk about their issues and concerns, that this might help them to get the protection that they need' (Skeels, 2014: 1).

Our shared approach has drawn on and built on these debates and perspectives and the important relationship between children and young people's best interests, protection and participation, positioned at the heart of the design and subsequent implementation of both studies. Through employing largely qualitative methodologies, a key premise has been that putting young people at the centre of knowledge production both recognises and holds the potential to realise their rights. Neither study has focused on the experiences of child abuse, maltreatment or exploitation that children and young people experienced during their journeys to and within the UK. Rather, both studies have been concerned with present and future planning, drawing out the current situations children found themselves in and what they wished to do with their lives, their aspirations and hopes for the future, although set within the limitations of the UK's legislative and policy environments detailed in Chapter 1.

Both studies in this book have also been concerned with what Jacobsen and Landau (2003) have called a 'dual imperative' in research to both satisfy high academic standards and ensure knowledge production improves the lives of people concerned, including by influencing policy and practice. The design of both studies has also been informed by feminist and postcolonial theory wherein knowledge is not separable from experience and is recognised as a 'historical product, produced in particular social, political and intellectual conditions', and which questions the nature of power in the production of knowledge (Ramazanoglu and Holland, 2002: 14).

As with any research study, there are limitations. For these two studies, the diverse and complex topic of human trafficking combined with engaging young people with a diverse range of experiences and backgrounds means that these studies cannot lay claim to generalisable findings for all young people affected by human trafficking in the UK. Of relevance here are UK-born children and young people increasingly significant in National Referral Mechanism (NRM) referrals each year but less directly included in these studies for a range of access, logistical and practical reasons. For example, only two of the 30 young people engaged in the ICTG study were UK-born. Further research to include these children and young people is warranted. As with much of the available literature on human trafficking, research is gleaned from those who are in receipt of services, or in touch with service providers, and young people in these studies were no exception (Brunovski and

Surtees, 2007). Those with no such contact are therefore not fully considered here.

Methods and ethics: a two-study reflection

We turn now to an overview and reflection on the aims, objectives, methods and ethical considerations involved in conducting the two studies with young people with lived experience of human trafficking.

Creating Stable Futures, human trafficking, participation and outcomes for children

The overarching aim of the Creating Stable Futures study was to understand positive outcomes from the perspectives of young people subjected to human trafficking, modern slavery and/or exploitation – and to consider what pathways towards these positive outcomes might look like in practice. A specific objective was to devise a young person-informed outcomes framework for the UK context, based on the knowledge and lived experiences of young people. Another objective was to ensure young people's views, knowledge and experiences regarding positive outcomes were brought into the centre of policy making, with suggestions for improvements and specific recommendations made for policy and practice. The four General Principles of the UNCRC were referred to as touchstones at each stage of this research. The full methodology from this 14-month study, conducted between September 2021 and October 2022 across England and Scotland, is available in full elsewhere (Hynes et al, 2022), as is a further explanation of the nature of international literature reviewed (Hynes, 2024). Here we outline the range of methods adopted which allowed for triangulation of sources in Table 2.1 (Denzin, 2017).

It is important to say that the workshops with young people were designed to reflect their rights under the UNCRC and ran alongside ethical considerations relayed later in this chapter.

Table 2.1: Summary of methods (CSF study)

Method	Details
Qualitative, participatory and arts-based research workshops with young people	20 workshops in 3 locations across England and Scotland with 31 young people across a range of nationalities and between 15 and 25 years old (April–June 2022)
Global call for practice evidence	Call made through ECPAT UK's international network in English, French, Spanish and Russian; responses from 8 countries
Systematic scoping review	UK and international peer-reviewed literature
Qualitative data analysis	Triangulation of sources and findings
Participatory workshops with young people	'Wrap up' workshops with young people to feedback on CSF-POF and verify findings

Key learning on this and the MS Outcomes study can be seen in a separate section later.

The global call for relevant national or international stakeholder evidence was made to ensure that practice-based evidence, often lacking in academic literature, was included. The key purpose of this call was to identify evidence on outcomes for young people who had experienced human trafficking within different contexts as well as to identify examples of children and young people's participation. Examples of practice, reports, policy briefs, evaluations and other resources relating to outcomes were invited; this led to responses from eight countries, including one from the Philippines involving a multi-stakeholder, co-research and co-design process to develop child-centred indicators for violence prevention (Third et al, 2020). This report detailed outcomes as describing how the world would look after a critical issue was resolved.

The scoping reviews focused on UK peer-reviewed literature on outcomes, an international review of systematic reviews on trafficking and trafficking-adjacent areas, plus the 'what works' evidence base across a range of trafficking and other cognate social issues. Systematic scoping reviews incorporate features of systematic review principles, processes and procedures to ensure a thorough, robust, reliable and transparent review process (Bryman, 2012). They are useful in 'reconnaissance' of literature, to both clarify working definitions and conceptual boundaries in complex or heterogenous bodies of literature (Peters et al, 2015). Here it is important to say that the UK-focused scoping revealed a small but growing body of research specifically on trafficked and/or exploited children This literature focuses on children's experiences of human trafficking, situations of vulnerability to trafficking, service responses, experiences of frontline and advocacy services as well as an emerging focus on retrafficking (Hynes, 2010, 2015; Kelly and Bokhari, 2012a, b; Pearce et al, 2013; Gearon, 2019; Hynes et al, 2022).

Internationally, the topics of human trafficking and modern slavery have seen research mainly emerging over the past two decades following the widespread uptake of the 2000 Trafficking Protocol (Gallagher, 2015b). Literature on trafficking is often exploratory, qualitative, predominantly descriptive, fragmented and lacking in prevalence or any accurate quantitative basis (Cockbain et al, 2018). As Cockbain et al outline, this literature is limited and dominated by reports from official agencies with peer-reviewed outputs comparatively rare. There are rich and nuanced accounts of human trafficking which form part of this young topic, but any critical appraisal of the evidence-base would also highlight how there is a lack of studies exploring the perspectives of those who have experienced trafficking and, in the case of the UK, are moving through support structures (Brodie et al, 2018).

One of the important findings in this review was the way it revealed a range of negative outcomes, negative health outcomes and negative consequences as a result of human trafficking as well as an overall lack of the views of children. It became clear that there is a significant gap in evidence relating to outcomes for children and young people post-trafficking, particularly literature that considers these from the perspective of children and young people themselves. Both aspects are pertinent to subsequent chapters in this book.

The use of different sources allowed for triangulation of findings and comparison across these different sources (Denzin, 2017). Qualitative accounts from young people and the results of the literature review and global call for practice evidence were analysed separately and then findings compared. Results of this analysis are detailed in subsequent chapters, including the development of a Creating Stable Futures Positive Outcomes Framework (CSF-POF) in Chapter 7, which resulted from analysis of sources both deductively (based around the aims of the research) and inductively (from the words and views of young people and post-thematic analysis of transcripts, photographs and other visual materials generated during workshops). This thematic analysis allowed for the development of 25 outcomes consistently arising from the suggestions of young people, grounded in their own language and experiences, which went on to inform the second study herein.

Outcomes for Children and Young People Affected by Modern Slavery: an analysis of ICTG service support in England and Wales

The main aim of the Outcomes for Children and Young People Affected by Modern Slavery study was to explore the benefits and limitations of the Independent Child Trafficking Guardianship (ICTG) service on outcomes for children and young people, their safeguarding, recovery, protection and well-being. The research aimed to situate this amid the nature of modern slavery affecting children in England and Wales and

Table 2.2: Summary of methods (MS Outcomes study)

Method	Details
Quantitative research – administrative data	NRM and ICTG service data 2017–22
Qualitative research – case data	10% ICTG case-closure summaries 2017–22
Qualitative research – focus group discussions (FGDs)	5 FGDs with regional teams of practitioners (56 in total) across ICTG service
Qualitative research – Q-methodology	Q-sorts with 30 young people aged 15–18 supported or having left the ICTG service
Qualitative data analysis	Use of 'Ken Q' package to analyse data from Q-methodology and data triangulation
Participatory workshops with additional Young People's Advisory Group	10 young people from the ICTG service participated in research design, analysis and dissemination

to set out what this might mean for policy and practice. The research used a suite of qualitative and quantitative methods to explore the cases, experiences and perspectives of children and young people supported by the ICTG service and for triangulation purposes, as shown in Table 2.2.

Q-methodology, or Q (Ellingsen et al, 2010; Thorsen and Størksen, 2010) is a participatory methodology with a statistical component which involves a 'Q-sort' where participants rank a set of statements relating to a single question on a grid according to their experiences or views. In this way, Q is used to draw out patterns, differences and consensus on a particular focus area where a range of perspectives are possible (Watts and Stenner, 2012). Q was deliberately selected for this study because it is considered effective for research participants who might find more traditional methods difficult and need a more interactive, shared activity, for topics or themes that are complex and/or sensitive, and for enabling participants to have more control over what they share and its interpretation.

The participation of ten young people with lived experience of modern slavery as 'young advisers' on the research, in addition to the young people engaged as research participants through Q, was at the centre of the research design, in keeping with a child-focused approach. Particular attention was given to data from young people's experiences and perspectives which was captured using Q-methodology, found in some case-closure summaries in ICTG service case files and communicated by proxy through practitioner focus groups, here prioritised as follows.

Ultimately, a set of 28 outcome statements was produced for the research, drawn mostly from the outcomes in the CSF-POF and co-adapted with young people. A total of 25 young people, each supported directly by a practitioner from the ICTG service, undertook a 'Q-sort' activity. Of these 25, 20 were male and 5 were female, all were aged between 15 and 18 and all had been supported by the ICTG service for between five and 29 months. Two of the young people were born in the UK and 23 were born outside the UK, including in Albania, Ethiopia, Vietnam, Sudan, Afghanistan, Brunei, Iraq, Gambia, and Guinea. None of these 23 young people had a 'figure of parental responsibility' in the UK.

As per the CSF study, the use of different sources allowed for triangulation of findings and comparison across these different sources (Denzin, 2017). Case-closure summaries contained qualitative information written by practitioners (case workers) at the point of children and young people's transition out of the ICTG service. A purposive sample of 10 per cent of ICTG 'cases' for the period from May 2017 to October 2022, 400 children in total, was identified and analysed in the research to examine outcomes reported for children and young people by ICTG workers upon case closure. Such data helped to describe children and young people's journeys over time through the service and revealed further nuance on how outcomes for children and young people had been supported, achieved, and understood. However, case-closure summaries did not represent a full picture of outcomes – in particular, from children and young people's own perspectives – nor could changes be solely attributed to ICTG service interventions given the number of professionals involved in these children's and young people's lives.

Five interactive, online sessions were held with ICTG service regional teams of practitioners (North, South, London, Midlands, and Wales), with 56 ICTG service staff participating. Focus group discussions can help to generate debate and discussion and result in rich data from multiple participants in a relatively short period of time. Practitioners engaging in the focus groups were asked to map the nature of child modern slavery based on their professional experience as well as to share how their roles impacted on outcomes for children and young people across a range of outcome areas. A total of 45 of the 56 ICTG service practitioners engaged in the regional focus group discussions also submitted their 'top five' outcome areas that they considered most important for children and young people in the service.

Key learning

These two studies resulted in several points of key learning when conducting participatory research with children and young people with lived experience of human trafficking, which included:

- accepting that planning participatory work with young people takes time and space to create social or interpersonal relationships of trust, within larger contexts where political or institutional trust may be missing and spaces for restoration of trust are lacking;
- working with partners with existing relationships with and understandings of what working with young people involves and who have a focus on rights was especially valuable;

- making children and young people's engagement in research inviting, welcoming, engaging, validating their unique contributions and skills and building their confidence, working within spaces of possibility and allowing space for young people to flourish, reflect and connect;
- ensuring the studies were child-centred and trauma-informed, using a 'toolkit' approach that incorporated a range of arts, talking, poetry, storytelling and multi-media activities: for example, the Young People's Advisory Group for the MS Outcomes study engaged a spoken word artist and poet to work with the young people and the researcher to analyse and share messages on the findings from the research;
- for the Creating Stable Futures study, ensuring the benefits of conducting workshops jointly run by an arts therapist and member of research staff, designed to create a safe and enabling space where informed consent to take part could be ensured from the outset;
- aiming to establish a participatory research process to work within 'spaces of possibility' with young people having the time and freedom to create, reflect and connect with other young people and the research team;
- accepting that young people involved had variable experiences of participation which meant workshops took differing rhythms across different locations, with some young people preferring simply to talk and others preferring other modes of expression;
- as a consequence, tailoring some activities more to young people's preferences: for example, in the MS Outcomes study and during the Q-sort activities, young people chose who to conduct this activity with, dependent upon their situation, safety and safety needs;
- ensuring young people felt listened to, which involved hearing what they wanted us to hear;
- understanding that it takes time for translation and interpretation not only of language, but also of concepts, ideas

and any power dynamics involved: using interpreters who young people are already familiar with works best, if possible;
- making sure that research was not being done 'for', 'on' or 'to' young people, but 'with' them;
- avoidance of reproducing exploitative environments or structured interviews which young people may have experienced in other settings and providing reassurances on anonymity;
- accepting that the workshops began on unequal ground in terms of rights held by the therapist, researchers and young people;
- accepting that participatory work is often conducted in ambiguous spaces where definition may be elusive, but such tensions are accepted as they emerge;
- not reducing young people to distinct characteristics such as their nationality and looking for more common ground, as well as respecting each individual's unique identity;
- working with an informed, committed and flexible funder; and
- importantly, ensuring that young people who take part see ways in which the research will be used.

These points of key learning were some of the ways in which safe spaces were created and adapted where necessary.

Ethical considerations

A range of implications for conducting ethical research arise out of studies with children, particularly in instances like these involving child maltreatment, abuse and exploitation. Children and young people who have been trafficked, albeit with different experiences, can be rendered vulnerable due to a range of contextual factors and consequences surrounding their trafficking and exploitation as well as their immigration status. As such, the two studies introduced here raised sensitive issues. While neither study focused on past and potentially traumatic experiences, young people did refer to these on occasion and it was therefore important to be prepared for this, anticipating possible harms.

A key strength of both studies was their access to pre-existing groups of young people, with recourse to safeguards and support from staff trained in trauma-informed and therapeutic approaches. This approach meant that there was available support for participants after their participation in workshops. In this way, concerns about the overprotection of groups of children in vulnerable situations who may be excluded from opportunities in research were overcome. As Stalford and Lundy (2022) have previously outlined in relation to children's rights to protection, participation and research ethics, such overprotection: 'inhibits efforts to interrogate and understand the world of the most marginalised from their own perspectives and, in turn, to explore, identify and evaluate appropriate responses to their needs' (2022: 892).

This consideration of ethics around children and young people's participation in research and any potential situations of vulnerability is very relevant to research with children and young people with lived experience of human trafficking, including those forcibly migrating to the UK. For example, in an international context, Lowicki (2002) suggests that it is 'absurd and belittling' to suggest that adolescents who have been subjected to war and 'thrust into adult roles prematurely' (for example, as soldiers, mothers, fathers, heads of households, husbands, wives, principal wage earners) with extremely limited support might not be able to participate in research. To move beyond this, Stalford and Lundy (2022) provide instances where child rights-based and trauma-informed approaches can be used to tackle these barriers so that children 'in the most vulnerable of circumstances' can still take part in research and be protected from additional harm. This more nuanced approach resonates with the two studies included in this book.

Ethical guidelines are emergent but as yet underdeveloped in respect of children and young people who experience trafficking or exploitation (Hynes and Dottridge, 2024). However, the ethos, methodology and principles of participatory research with children can mitigate many of these complex ethical concerns. Ensuring that the research is conducted ethically, with responsibility towards participants and carried out in ways that underpin confidence in results is always essential (Jacobsen and Landau, 2003; Carling, 2019).

Key principles and strategies for conducting this type of research safely and ethically and engaged by these two studies include:

- children and young people having control over the topics and issues being discussed;
- all participants being free to withdraw their participation from the research at any time, with this right to withdraw being clearly communicated to all participants verbally and confirmed in writing as part of the 'informed consent' process;
- negotiating informed consent through age-specific, language-appropriate and detailed information sheets and informed consent forms, with audio or visual back up made available for those with limited literacy and interpreters used who have good practice standards;
- confidentiality, guarantees of and best practices to protect anonymity, and full explanations of the limits to confidentiality;
- clear outlines of the risks and benefits of participating in research;
- respect for children's competencies to understand and explain their worlds and propose solutions to problems encountered;
- addressing disparities of power between adults and children through relational principles and approaches;
- adopting procedures for disclosure that prioritise child protection responsibilities if abuse and/or potential significant harm is disclosed, while acknowledging that young people will have views on ways to proceed based on their own experiences;

- ensuring a fair return and recognition for research engagement with all participants;
- ensuring all data is collated and stored in accordance with data protection legislation; and
- ensuring distress to research team members is minimised and their safety ensured.

Full research ethics approvals were sought from the university research ethics committees of both universities involved in these studies. An iterative approach was also taken to everyday ethics and issues arising, ensuring flexibility and adaptability with children and young people.

Conclusion

Reflecting on the shared approach of the two studies forming the focus of this book, it's clear that the ethical participation of children and young people who have lived experience of trafficking, exploitation and/or modern slavery in research takes time and requires a particular set of circumstances and support to do well. Time to plan carefully, to create and open spaces for trust, translation and interpretation is vital. Collaborating with partners with existing understandings of what working with young people involves and who have a focus on rights is especially valuable in this regard, as is working with an advisory group of young people. Supportive funders are also key.

While not an explicit aim of the CSF study, we found that when young people were listened to, believed and had their views given due weight, there was an implicit understanding that relationships being built involved some forms of often unspoken reciprocity. While contact time with young people for the study on the ICTG service was more limited, a similar approach still enabled a relationship to be built. Both studies found that children and young people's participation in research had to be inviting, engaging, welcoming, work within spaces of possibility, and allow space for young people to flourish, reflect and connect. Spaces that allow freedom to create and allow children to express themselves are key. Listening and ensuring young people see ways in which the research will be used are equally important.

This chapter has outlined the methods, shared approach and ethical considerations of our two studies. Turning now to the context we were working within, we move to the first of four findings chapters reflecting on the UNCRC's General Principles. The first of these, Article 2 on non-discrimination, details the environment in which the research was conducted, outlining some of the many broader barriers to participation that the young people engaged in the research were experiencing.

THREE

Non-discrimination in principle and practice

Introduction

I used to go every single day to the social worker's office talking with the guy, with … the manager of the social workers. 'Why don't you just go back to your country?' That's what he say. (2022)

A good system of equality from the government. We are talking about giving people their documents on time. … Some people are waiting for so long. (2022)

So, you feel like, for years, you don't get your documentation, you'll be treated just like an animal. (2022)

Because our voice [needs] to be heard and what we're saying to be the exact same [as] what they're translating and not cause any problems in the future because a lot of people might have had a lot of problems because of wrong translation and it's very important for their future.

So, it's not a joke, the application that they're doing. So, it's their life basically, so it's very important. (2022)

When you are like, say, age 17, 18, your thinking is then all about 'my status, my status' because then you can't go to university without papers, you can't even go to college. Some college[s] turn me down. (2022)

We now turn to the context within the UK in which this research was carried out, detailing what young people said about the many formal and informal exclusions through which they had faced discrimination or felt discriminated against. The focus of this chapter is Article 2 of the United Nations Convention on the Rights of the Child (UNCRC) on non-discrimination which details how: 'The Convention applies to every child without discrimination, whatever their ethnicity, gender, religion, language, abilities or any other status, whatever they think or say, whatever their family background.' This Article sets out to ensure all children have the same rights, without discrimination of any kind. When the United Kingdom ratified the UNCRC in 1991, it entered a general reservation to Article 22 of the Convention with regards to immigration and nationality, excluding children subject to immigration control. This was removed in 2008 by the then Labour Government, bringing the UK closer to ensuring these rights must be applied to all children without discrimination.

The views of the young people detailed in the opening quotes provide an insight into how this principle works in practice in the UK. These young people discussed the systems and processes they found themselves in, how these were shaped by the attitudes of professionals around them, the importance of documentation and what they considered needed to change for this universal right to equality – or non-discrimination – for both themselves and others, to be realised in practice as well as principle.

Some of the young people in the CSF study understood their rights and entitlements under UK law, others had hazier understandings based on encounters with professionals and practitioners who worked with them. These young people, without anyone present in the UK with parental responsibility, counted on professionals to act in ways that made them feel safe.

This chapter will now explore in more depth what young people from our two studies told us that reflects the realities of their lives in relation to non-discrimination and Article 2. We draw on first-hand accounts – such as those at the start of this chapter – of how and to what extent this general principle is reflected in their lived experiences. We share rich and nuanced empirical material generated by young people during their repeat engagement in the CSF study and from the MS Outcomes study with young survivors reflecting on their experiences of ICTG service support.

Questions relating to interpretation, translation and language abilities were mainly evident in the CSF study. Questions around trust, however, were evident in both studies. It is in this chapter that we begin to see how age and the transition to 'adulthood' at 18 was an anxiety-riven period for many young people encountered in the CSF research. Young people engaged in the second study seemed to feel this anxiety less keenly, were more informed about their rights, supported and confident about getting older. In the CSF study, freedoms – from gender discrimination, the ability to practise a chosen religion and find peace – in relation to the many 'unfreedoms' (Sen, 1999) experienced, were discussed.

Impact of asylum and immigration procedures: 'I am believed'

Central to any consideration of refugee and asylum-seeking young people's lives, including those affected by human trafficking, is a now well-rehearsed and well-documented narrative around the negative impacts of immigration and asylum procedures. Legislation and policy towards people who migrate has been framed within a 'hostile environment' and, as Clayton et al (2021) suggest, this 'hostility also arguably affects those who are required to administer the increasing number of internal immigration controls' in their day-to-day interactions (2021: 58). Yuval-Davis et al (2019) have also argued that the concept of borders and bordering has moved from the margins into the very centre of political and social life. This, combined with the lack of alternative safe routes into the UK, makes the context into which young people arrive and in which they then live precarious for them.

These narratives spill out across a broader population, including to those working alongside children and young people. As Chase and Allsopp suggest in relation to young people, 'the bordered realities of their becoming' (2021: 135) impact on their ability to realise the types of futures they aspire to when approaching adulthood, particularly their uncertain legal status, and require a focus on their precarity – in particular the 'politically-induced' nature of their precariousness (Butler, 2006, cited in Chase and Allsopp, 2021).

In the CSF study, young people identified barriers to reaching positive outcomes as structural, systemic and discriminatory. This included their experiences of immigration and asylum systems, the criminal justice system, and support during their time in the care system. The young people involved in the study outlined ways in which they considered such structural inequalities shaped professional practice and attitudes towards them. During the MS Outcomes study, ICTG service practitioners engaged in the research also spoke in detail about the hostile political environment and structural barriers faced by young people in the immigration system and the frustrations involved.

This feeling resonated across different groups in the CSF study, with discussions around how a lack of documentation or legal status had the effect of pulling young people backwards in their lives:

> Because that pulls you back. You need to have that document. We all have potential, we all have a future

career, so when you don't have the document, you can't do that. ... And a friend of mine last year, [football team in UK], all the bigger teams, came for him. And he had to pull out because of his documents. He called the Home Office and they said, 'We don't know when we're going to say that, it could be two years'. He was 17 and he is 18, 19 I think, so that's what I'm talking about. They are not going to wait for you. (2022)

The relationship between documentation and moving towards a feeling of independence was ever present during this study's workshops:

The document will give you your world, will make you more independent, to actually have your own place, you can go work as an independent person. (2022)

These themes were in places reiterated in the MS Outcomes study, with one young person describing how he felt he had been treated by the Home Office regarding his age on arrival in the UK:

In the first meeting, they decide my age. They didn't listen to me. That reason I have been in the very bad situation for nine months. (2023)

Running through these accounts were reflections on a sometimes default response of disbelief – about their account or age – making young people feel unsafe and adding to their feelings of being in some way unequal to others.

Perceptions of equality and inequality: 'I am treated equally to other children in the UK'

Equality – and this perception of inequality – was repeatedly highlighted by young people, with equality ultimately becoming an important outcome in and of itself in the CSF study, with discussions echoing the UNCRC's focus on opportunities, fair treatment and rights. Young people spoke about the 'rules' and 'opportunities' feeling 'different' for them when they compared themselves to UK-born children:

> There's different opportunities for asylum-seekers and British UK ... (2022)

Young people engaged in the second study and navigating immigration procedures similarly pointed out the 'rules' around, or limitations to, their access to opportunities in the UK, for example, in relation to education:

> Because of his situation in the system, he can't choose any subject he wants to learn. (2023)

Plus, in response to an outcome statement in the second study about 'I can achieve things', a young person reiterated this inequality through his interpreter:

> He says, there are limits to what he can achieve because of his circumstances. (2023)

Other young people in the CSF study referred directly to the UNCRC Articles, such as Article 22:

> For equality: refugee, asylum-seeker and British people, child, there is an Article 22 that says equality of education, equality of job, we're talking about that. (2022)

Another young person said simply:

> Everyone needs to be equal. (2022)

When not referring to immigration procedures, young people engaged in the MS Outcomes study responded positively to the statement: 'People treat me similarly to other young people my age.' In most cases, this was in reference to their treatment by and belief in the ICTG service:

> Yeah. Pretty sure you're going to be doing the same thing you do with me [with] other young people of my age. (2023)

Others questioned how they could know definitively whether other young people were being treated the same as them or considered whether differential treatment might be important in some cases, depending on young people's individual needs:

> I don't know how one can understand 'I'm treated similarly to others', everybody have their own way of feeling. (2023)

> Timing for example, sometimes a young person needs like 80 per cent, 75 per cent help from others and sometimes some young people can do a lot for themselves. (2023)

The ICTG service, then, it seems, creates or negotiates a more equal and less discriminatory environment for these young people in some ways, albeit within a broader structurally hostile immigration system and context within the UK, which becomes more important as young people approach transitioning out of the service at 18.

'My culture, religion and identity are respected' and 'I am able to have an interpreter when I need one'

In relation to culture, religion and identity, in particular, young people engaged in the MS Outcomes study mostly felt that they had had their different and unique needs respected and met by the ICTG service. Here, we learn about young people's perceptions of equality, inequality and inclusion in this second study from their response to the outcome statement 'my culture, religion and identity are respected':

> And she kept asking me questions, wanting to know whether anything she could do to help me about my religion and culture … for example, I had a photo of Buddha hanging on my wall and she said, oh anything else she could get for me in order for me to worship my religion and she took time to ask me how I practise my religion. (2023)

> I agree with the support I have received here about my religion. My religion is being respected here. … For example, when I came here, it was Ramadan and I have been supported fully … they help me a lot. When, for example, on Friday I wanted to go to mosque, so they don't make an appointment on Friday. So, they respected my times. (2023)

Young people spoke about how their ICTGs had helped them to access appropriate places of worship:

> I remember I said I didn't know where the mosque was and then she showed me, like, around. (2023)

> I am a Catholic and they gave me the opportunity to go to church. (2023)

Not all young people had yet received such support, however, with one young person flagging:

> Cultural religion is very important for me, very crucial. But in the meantime, I did not receive help or support from the organization. (2023)

A key part of this was access to interpreters and translation, but also peer support that was safe and appropriate:

> In the beginning when I arrived, it was very difficult for me to understand the people here and the living

culture and style and everything. ... I was given the opportunity by the worker to give me somebody who would be from Afghanistan and who could help me make this process of understanding the life and culture here. (2023)

Oh yes, yes, definitely, because you know, every time when you take me out, you always make sure that there's something printed in Vietnamese so that I can fully understand. (2023)

Young people in the CSF study commented on and made suggestions around interpreters, about how there should be child-specific interpreters available whose training should include safeguarding, being trauma-informed and knowing how to speak to children:

So well-trained interpreter for everyone. ... Maybe get interpreters which are only for young people. Be nice and kind and explain like two, three times, give them their time to explain, ask, 'If you did understand?'. You know, treat them like a friend from your country and just explain slowly and nicely so the person feels comfortable to share as well, because it's very difficult for you to share with a person from your own country. (2022)

There has been a long-standing lack of interpreters who speak the same dialect as young people claiming their right to asylum from persecution, and consistency of interpreters was also raised in the CSF study, particularly in relation to Home Office interviews that could make or break asylum applications.

The significance of missing educational opportunities

Educational opportunities were significant for young people in both studies and in relation to a sense of equality and non-discrimination. The significance of missing education was highlighted, including young people not having the same access to student finance, further education, higher education and/or apprenticeships and was a clear motif throughout the CSF study. One young person captures these inequalities succinctly:

> The disappointment is education. And the support needed is equal access to student finance without being discriminated [against] ... so the support is educational, [having a] social worker, giving young people alternative ... apprenticeships as well, it's not just about focusing on only schools and things like that. And the last support I feel is part-time job or work experience as well. (2022)

This disappointment related directly to formal exclusions from student finance was repeated by others. There were several instances where young people talked about missing educational opportunities due to their lack of legal status, having to 'wait' in the asylum system, and how they felt somehow 'stuck' due to the ongoing denial of access to all forms of education:

> You're missing out, you're missing education ... asylum-seekers, they can't go to university, and they ... study part-time in college. This needs to change because they want to study and they might get papers a year later, they're just wasting a year and wasting some modules ... it's not fair just because you're waiting for an answer you can't do full-time course, or you can't go to uni. (2022)

Young people highlighted the benefits of education and the potential positive impact it held for their lives throughout the CSF study:

> So, if we ... study some still while doing English we're not feeling stuck, we're able to get more jobs. (2022)

A lot of young people spoke about success, accomplishments and being allowed to have a second life but there was an awareness that there were limits to the levels of education they could access:

> Let just speak about the possibilities. If you're an asylum-seeker, you want to go to a university, that is not going to happen unless you have your decision from the Home Office. You know, that is the one thing that is really struggling for some of us. (2022)

> I've done two years in that college already, my third year in that college ... I am telling you seriously like, it make you go mad. So, if literally someone said do this two-year route, and said he is going back, then just give his documents and straightaway there will be mad, seriously, because the stress of documents can make you go mad. It doesn't matter who you are, you are an immigrant. (2022)

For a young person to refer to themselves as 'an immigrant' in this way reveals undertones of racism experienced, which authors such as Solomos have shown to be 'the outcome of complex political, social and economic processes' relating to 'race' and racism (Solomos, 1989: 175). The association with the known lens of immigration as detailed in Chapter 1 is also striking.

Some of the young people engaged in the second study also pointed out the 'rules', or limitations, to their access to education in the UK. Young people engaged in the research on the ICTG service talked about education and its significance for them: 'education is very, very, important. Very crucial for my life' (2023). Importantly, 21 out of the 25 young people involved in the second study agreed with statement 'I can have the education I need' as a result of support from the ICTG service: 'Yeah, I received education I need, and I agree with that' (2023); 'people take his education and college seriously and check how he is doing and support him and his education' (2023); 'In Vietnam, he didn't receive good care or education but better in UK and taken care of and [ICTG worker] helped him to go to high school and then college and access ESOL [English for speakers of other languages] tuition online' (2023).

Some young people also spoke about small acts that they related to supporting their education, for example, their support worker giving them a dictionary or 'teaching important information about life in the UK' (2023). These everyday encouragements from the ICTGs had significant impact on the lives of young people.

Some young people had also been supported in accessing education by adults other than their ICTG service direct worker, for example, by their foster carers or social workers, but felt confident that they would also be supported in this by the ICTG service in the future if needed: 'I was at college before Barnardo's. But if I want to access education, Barnardo's will help me' (2023).

Educational opportunities are also explored in Chapter 5, where they are considered as being part of child development.

Professional attitudes

Across the three locations of the CSF study, a strong message emerged from young people about the unjust treatment they experienced, setting them apart from other children and young people they met. Young people outlined ways in which they considered how the more structurally based inequalities they were encountering could shape professional practice and attitudes towards them. Young people also offered accounts of what they saw as explicitly framed discriminatory and sometimes racist attitudes from those with a duty to safeguard and ensure their best interests. For example, one 16-year-old, who had been age-assessed incorrectly and was requesting to be moved from age-inappropriate shared accommodation with adults, found that professionals were unwilling to help despite serious risks he had raised with them:

> Since 16, my social workers they put me with an adult, they have like 54 and 45 [years] and they used to bring friends, like 20 friends in the house. (2022)

In the view of this young person, this lack of care and the dangers involved in being accommodated inappropriately came from the professional involved being in their role for payment rather than being 'in love' with their job:

> Some social workers they just do it for the business. (2022)

This was a recurrent theme from young people engaged in the CSF research:

> Some people, they do the job, but I don't think they love their jobs because they just [pause] not very friendly, I think. Like to be a support worker or to be a key worker or to be a social worker, they have to be patient, friendly and good listener and they have to love the job. (2022)

Other young people repeated this and what it meant for the services young people would then ultimately receive:

> So I think for professionals when they actually love you they will go that extra mile to make sure they get you sorted. (2022)

Among young people in the CSF study, there were mixed views on their experiences with social workers. Some had clearly developed trusting relationships with social workers who gave them support when needed:

> Trust, trust is 100 per cent very important. I trust with her so much, I would share any problem with her and she would support me with that and give me advice. ... And also, all my information she gave me, I shared to my friends and to the group that I volunteer. So, she didn't only help me but helped a lot of other people through me. (2022)

Other young people described their interactions at the other end of this scale, or spoke about friends who had social workers that were more distant and uncaring or outwardly displayed stress during interactions:

> And I have so many other friends, they don't even know their social worker or they just have their number for maybe money support or for their applications for college ... they don't go to visit them. They try to push them to move to their [own] house as soon as possible so they don't deal with them anymore or they just say, 'Oh, hi, how are you doing?', and then fill their papers there, that, 'Oh, we've been in contact with this young person and he's doing great. They've got their own house, blah-blah-blah.' (2022)

Young people also commented on the attitudes of staff working in their accommodation, referring to them as being helpful:

> She take me to the [supermarket] for the shopping the first time. I buy like, you know, everything like. And then we go back home and she started to cook with me and she tried to chat with me and she do a lot of things to make you laugh to get me the mood where I come from to be like comfortable and then I start my life, you know, like that. (2022)

But the same staff were also considered as needing training around trauma and better understanding of young people's circumstances. A distinction for young people between 'good' and 'bad' foster carers was also evident by their approach, sensitivity and willingness to provide support, for example, of 'unaccompanied children':

> I said a good foster carer because for me to use the phrase, 'good', which means not everyone out there are good. (2022)

Other professionals' attitudes, such as the police, solicitors and interpreters, were also recounted. As one young person suggested, the police needed to be 'well-trained' and 'not just the normal police that deal with criminals' (2022). Encounters with police officers ranged from being scary, 'horrible' (2022) and taking time to realise that 'police here and back home are quite different' (2022):

> I had an interview with one of the ladies and I think she was from police ... but she was very, very like 'make you feel scared' even though you didn't do anything. So angry, so not nice or kind or anything. She'll just be like, 'There's the camera, here's the mic and then you talk now and you must answer every single question that I tell you otherwise you have to come here again'. (2022)

There were also accounts from young people of the everyday bordering roles the police undertake:

> I'm going to come in on something he said, it's actually right because we have an incident and we went to the police, the first thing that they are gonna tell you, is 'Are you in this country legally?', if you are not legal so, 'You have to be legal before we can do something'. ... 'Is your passport still not ready?', 'Yes', 'So there's nothing we can do.' They just literally left, so yeah ... (2022)

Overall, a lack of care in some cases and young people distinguishing between 'good' and 'bad' care were recurrent responses. Many young people felt as though professionals working with them were uncaring about their situations or did not have sufficient training and understanding about their lives.

ICTGs engaged in the second study also spoke a lot about the attitudes and practices of other professionals, for example, social workers and the police, in relation to children and young people affected by human trafficking and how these could be unhelpful or present barriers to their protection. Indeed, part of the role of the ICTG is to raise awareness of the challenges faced and needs of children and young people affected by human trafficking with other professionals. The attitudes and practices of ICTGs themselves, as experienced by young people engaged in our research, were in most cases in contrast to that of other professionals, and this is explored further in Chapter 4.

'I can access high quality care'

Young people spoke about how professionals should work with them and treat them in ways that made them feel safe, and safe enough to discuss their lives and share information with them. As one young person outlined, this could be 'one person' who stands by them:

> Someone that can stand for you, you know like probably a foster carer, social worker, somebody that, when you have any issues, others aren't there to help you but that one person that will always be there for you, stand for you. (2022)

Another young person spoke about the many differences they had experienced within the care system and how 'one person' had changed their views:

> I've had a lot of terrible support workers so I can really tell and differentiate when someone actually loves

you, my PA [personal adviser] treat me like her own child. ... They show you sympathy, empathy because they are actually trying to feel what you are feeling at that point, so because the best way for you to help someone, you have to put yourself in that position .... (2022)

Another young person commented on changes needed across a broader range of professionals:

It's not just about the foster care because the teachers, social workers, everyone who knows the child didn't really look for him. We need to change lots of people! (2022)

This was a subject taken up with one group of young people who wrote an article for *Children & Young People Now*[1] detailing what they wanted social workers, personal advisers, healthcare professionals, lawyers and foster carers to know and how they could make a difference in their lives. This included the professionals supporting them to find a home, practical issues, access to well-trained interpreters, access to education, healthcare and/or training as well as guiding them through complicated and confusing immigration and other processes. For foster carers they suggested that:

When young people turn 18, they don't become a different person – an adult who doesn't need any support at all. For many of us, age categories determine the kind of care we receive. Some of us have been treated like strangers by our foster carers as soon as we turn 18. New rules for interaction are introduced, and we are no longer included as part of the family. We need foster carers to remember that 18 is merely a number, and it comes to describe us in the space of a single day. (2022)

Other young people in the CSF study commented on what they needed in the care system and when:

> The first thing is protection. What ... I mean protection, for example, he must be safe. He must be safe and then he gets accommodation or house and then education and healthcare and friend. These five things. I mean, like, in the short term. ... Very important. And then what's next, he's supposed to have like guardianship or social worker and lawyer and translator – interpreter, sorry. ... Yeah. Interpreter I think is the first because he need interpreter for the first. So, interpreter is anywhere until he get to school or anything like that. (2022)

It was clear changes are needed for children and young people affected by human trafficking to access the quality of care they need. Too many had experienced professionals who did not support them and a more compassionate approach was part of discussions young people held. As noted earlier, young people, however, mostly experienced care from ICTGs differently and more positively compared to other professionals and this is explored further in Chapter 4.

Conclusion

> Because how you going to protect me if I don't trust you? (2022)

Historically, children have not always been seen or accepted as holders of rights, but as possessions of parents or as an economic resource and viewed as citizens-in-the-making, future citizens or human 'becomings' rather than as human 'beings' in their own right (Chase and Allsopp, 2021). The UNCRC, plus other international actions to consider children as active agents, has contributed to a changing view of children as being rights holders in their own right (Pinheiro, 2006).

Looking through the lens of non-discrimination across our two studies, there are areas of alignment as well as difference. Both studies include accounts from young people on the negative impacts of immigration procedures and routine barriers faced to full inclusion, although ICTG service support acted as a strong and positive contrast to this for those young people engaged. Young survivors participating in the CSF study had a strong perception of inequality in the treatment they felt they received, often experienced through the attitudes of professionals, compared to other children in the UK.

It is clear from the empirical material provided in this chapter that, for young people migrating to the UK with lived experience of human trafficking, the principle of non-discrimination as contained in Article 2 of the UNCRC is variably realised. Perceived inequalities in young people's everyday encounters with professionals form a key message coming from these studies. It was revealing that young people's experiences of feeling inequalities were largely experienced through the attitudes of professionals they encountered, although young people did also speak about professionals who provided good quality support – specifically those often seen as enjoying or loving their jobs in some way – for example, Guardians, where these were in place. Negative impacts of immigration narratives, procedures and subsequent barriers to full inclusion were relayed by young people and connected to the ways in which professional attitudes often reinforced their feelings of discrimination. Feedback from young people engaged in the second study, which focused on the ICTG service, reinforces this experience of Guardians as trusted adults whose attitudes and work reinforces principles of equality and non-discrimination and have a positive impact on young people's lives. This is explored further in the next chapter, Chapter 4.

Young people across the two studies discussed changes they saw as necessary across professions for their lives and the lives of others to improve now and in the future. This often focused on that 'one person' who would stand by them, support them, when necessary, guide them through complex processes and treat them well and with respect rather than discrimination.

FOUR

In whose best interests?

Introduction

I had to keep telling my story over and over again. … Why do we need to keep telling the same story again and again and again? (2022)

You are not able to determine your future … even if you're able to progress to your future, or not. But once you have your documents, that is a relief whereby your future is for you to determine. Not other people determine your future. Like making decisions about the future. We can make a decision about the future. (2022)

I can choose by myself because some things I know what's the best for me. And sometimes when I don't know, of course you can choose for me. (2023)

For you to actually pursue your dream as a young person, in this country, you need to be stable, for you to be stable, you need your documents. (2022)

This chapter focuses on Article 3 of the United Nations Convention on the Rights of the Child (UNCRC) on the 'best interests' of children. This General Principle details how the best interests of the child must be prioritised in all decisions and actions affecting children as outlined in Article 3(1): 'In all actions concerning children, whether undertaken by public or private social welfare institutions, courts of law, administrative authorities or legislative bodies, the best interests of the child shall be a primary consideration.' The best interests of children as a primary consideration thus applies to social workers, doctors, health professionals, social care workers, education professionals, independent guardians and those working within the full range of public or private institutions as detailed in this definition. Linking these best interests to protection and care, Article 3(2) details how State Parties must:

> … undertake to ensure the child such protection and care as is necessary for his or her well-being, taking into account the rights and duties of his or her parents, legal guardians, or other individuals legally responsible for him or her, and, to this end, shall take all appropriate legislative and administrative measures.

An obligation to ensure institutions, services and facilities then conform with standards then follows. However, as can be seen from the quotes in this chapter, young people in our studies felt their best interests could become lost within the formal systems and processes with which they had to engage. These often required them to spend months or years awaiting a decision on their legal status, to retell their accounts again and again to a range of professionals and, in doing so, feel both pulled back from making decisions about their own lives and the detrimental effects on their mental health. This raises a key question about whose best interests are being served here.

The principle of best interests provides protection for children and young people. However, it has been critiqued, particularly in UK and European policies, when it justifies the long-term best interests of young people being 'best served through their return to their countries of origin' (Chase and Allsopp, 2021: 132; see also Anderson, 2012; Allsopp and Chase, 2019).

Human rights can come 'from above' through such state obligations or 'from below' through the actions or inclusion of people with lived experience, be they within or outside civil society organisations (Nash, 2012). For most of the young people in our two studies, the absence of a figure of parental responsibility in the UK means that the state becomes their 'legitimate protector' (Anderson, 2012: 1253) requiring them to interact with a range of adults for their ongoing protection, for gaining legal status and meeting their support needs. Some of these adults in, for example, social care, will represent the state with roles that embody where the state meets the street (Lipsky, 2010; see also Sundbäck, 2024). Their working time may be scarce, affecting their encounters with young people and the ability to develop 'trusting relationships' (Sundbäck, 2024).

In this chapter, we explore what young people 'from below' prioritised in terms of their best interests, feeling cared for and having their needs met. From talking with these young people, we suggest that the protection of children under Article 3 should not be detrimental to their participation and their ability to express their views and have these taken into account, under Article 12, given consideration later in this book. This tension is explored in this chapter, with the rights of young people centred throughout.

As in Chapter 3, empirical material generated from young people during the CSF and MS Outcomes studies is outlined, providing first-hand accounts of how the best interests principle is reflected in their lived experience and in policy and practice.

'I am not left waiting for my immigration status'

Previous chapters have already discussed the impact of asylum and immigration procedures on young people and the feelings of inequality these provoked. The CSF study realised early on that obtaining legal status and documentation was clearly essential for young people to be able to feel truly protected, secure and safe.

Young people engaged in the CSF study did not feel it was in their best interests to be left waiting for legal status. There was a clearly articulated need for them to receive such status in a reasonable timeframe with the necessary support around them in the interim. This was repeatedly outlined, for example, by one young person who detailed gaining status as 80 per cent of their concerns; for another in the same workshop, this was even higher:

> I would say 90 per cent! I mean, imagine, when you are in this country and you are studying, and you are not sure with your status, it's going to be yes or no, are you going to fight for me? Is your lawyer still going to be there for you? You're not sure. (2022)

Gaining legal status was considered a gateway and foundation to other necessary services and also for young people to be able to move forward with their lives:

> When you have your document, it allows you to access the other things as well because ... getting your document is the primary objective which you just need to fix, whatever you're doing. (2022)

> You are going to have to start with your documents. (2022)

Young people talked about 'the struggle' and 'struggles' to gain protection and move forward, sometimes intricately bound up with educational opportunities, as detailed in Chapter 3:

> Yeah, I feel like it was true to me because, like, whenever you need something, you need to get it [documentation]

because, for example, to get the BSc you need to go to university, so if you need that kind of protection, you need to go for it, struggle for it, so those are the kind of struggles that you need to go through in order to get protected. So, what stood out to me about this though was, like, while I am waiting, you can wait for years in order to get the documents but it's worth fighting for what we want. (2022)

This was also connected with a recurring theme of having to wait for long periods, often years, for this status and needing to struggle to gain the protections others were able to access. Feelings of inequality and resulting uncertainty and the impacts this involved were apparent throughout. It was clear this necessity to wait for years had a considerable impact on their mental health:

But what about people that have been waiting for so long. ... They do not know where they are. (2022)

As detailed within the quotes at the start of this chapter, young people disliked having to tell the same 'story over and over again', repeating details about their past lives to achieve documentation and access the services they needed. Across the full range of professionals and practitioners described by these young people, the need to present an account of their experiences – of exploitation, of the ways they arrived into the UK, and their movement within the UK – was something they struggled with. Most recalled how these repeat encounters reopened traumatic memories, setting them back in terms of their recovery. In Home Office interviews, health settings, and other interviews and encounters with professionals, young people described this need to recall and retell:

And they said that kind of about the GPs, you know? That's when they said not just the Home Office and the

GPs, but we have to tell all these people the same story over and over again. (2022)

The ICTG service study included both UK-born and non-UK-born young people and was focused on young people's experience of the service. As a result, it did not always involve a consideration of the immigration and asylum systems by the young people engaged. As such, an outcome statement for these young people to respond to on 'Important decisions about my life are made quickly' was felt more appropriate. As a result, whereas in the CSF study young people brought up and discussed the systems and processes they found themselves in, in the MS Outcomes study, they spoke less about specific systems, procedures or documentation, and more about whether making important decisions quickly or slowly was best for them and their lives.

'I have good quality legal representation'

In both the CSF and MS studies, getting good quality legal advice relating to immigration, asylum, public and criminal law featured heavily in the accounts of young people. This included access to family reunification, relating to the right to having their family with them in the UK or – in more complex circumstances and/or in relation to UK-born young people – being able to have safe contact with their family if desired.

Part of the process of gaining legal status required high quality legal advice, identified by young people as a defining factor in determining outcomes in their lives. As detailed, gaining legal status was of central importance, with getting papers underpinning many areas of their lives. Legal status was in itself a foundational outcome, allowing young people to have hope and aspirations and to move forward with their lives. The ability to gain good quality legal advice across a range of complex social care, immigration and criminal justice systems featured heavily and the best interests of children and young people were best served when this type of legal advice was available to them.

Young people participating in the CSF study presented a mixed picture of solicitors and legal representation as a whole. Some outlined how they had received good legal advice, while others had needed to change solicitors during their time in the UK. In the MS Outcomes study, ICTGs had limited control over supporting young people to obtain good quality legal representation, both because of a national shortage of such legal advice and because young people sometimes joined the service with solicitors already in place. In cases where better legal representation was necessary, ICTGs helped young people to find this.

Young people in the CSF study raised issues such as solicitors cancelling appointments at the last minute, with a few commenting on how disruptive this was for them when they had prepared their paperwork in advance. Young people commented on the number of appointments they required:

> Why do I have to have 11 appointments with the solicitor? It's so much ... like it was really draining. (2022)

Other young people responded to this by again making a distinction between 'good' and 'bad' solicitors based on their approaches towards young people. Young people also occasionally outlined how their cases had been damaged in the past by poor quality legal representation, causing them considerable hardship and distress. Given the detail and thoroughness required to submit their papers, entailing the ongoing need for solicitors and associated professionals, young people were conscious and aware that success was dependent on the level of detail involved:

> And if they find a little space where they can catch you, they just get you and they say, 'Oh, you've got this specific thing that you didn't cover in your case, so we just give

you a negative answer'. And then you have to challenge them through the court, and to go through the court obviously you're going to need the help of guardians and solicitors and social workers because you don't know how it works in this country. (2022)

Young people wanted 'good' legal representatives who would 'fight' for them, making the connection between protection under the law and the need for good quality provision. Good quality legal representation was not, however, always something they experienced.

'I have people I can trust who support me': the introduction of Independent Child Trafficking Guardians (ICTGs)

The introduction of ICTGs is a key intervention shaping practice towards young people with lived experience of human trafficking (see Chapter 1 for background). In both studies, young people with access to ICTGs, or some other form of independent advocate, felt listened to, supported and heard, enabling their better protection These young people wanted to be kept informed about what was happening to them and its implications for their lives. The CSF study took place in parts of England where ICTGs or advocates were not always present and in Scotland where they were, but the MS Outcomes study focused exclusively on the ICTG service in England and Wales. The MS Outcomes study considers young people's perspectives on and lived experience of support from what they considered to be trusted adults within this service, whose role is to work in their best interests.

Because of the differing focus of our studies, a qualitative difference became apparent during joint analysis of our two data sets, based on the presence or absence of ICTGs. For example, during CSF workshops with young people and throughout the MS Outcomes study, it became clear that having access to trusted adults who either were informal advocates or recognised ICTGs was beneficial in the lives of young people. In contrast to the professionals' attitudes and practice outlined in Chapter 3, young people detailed how Guardians made them feel more comfortable, as a different kind of professional with a better way of relating to young people:

> And then finally ... I become very comfortable, they bring me a Guardianship and he was very nice person. And firstly when he come and I have dealt with him and I'm very happy because the way he talk with me and the way he ask me, he give me more chance and he give me more confidence, he just like talk with me like my friend or something like, maybe it could be your father or your brother or something like that, you know? (2022)

A key part of this was the way in which advocates or independent guardians listened to and spoke to young people, creating and maintaining appropriate and healthy relationships with them:

> The Guardian I think is really important for young people ... they have like special experience with young people. Even the way they talk to the young people or the way – that's really, really important and really special. They listen to the young people and they give you advice and they help you if you have any problem or if you need any help, they are able to help you at any time. For example, now I'm not under Guardianship care anymore but I think now if I have a big problem, I'll contact with my Guardianship firstly and my social worker. Yeah, so it's very important. (2022)

This was also clear in the second study:

> So, I was in this place, a very bad place for a very long time. Three years. And when [ICTG worker] started working with me, he made me feel calm. He took me out. He

talked to me, he listened to me. That was very important. That he listened to me and believed in me and that made me feel as if I am important. And not the way that I was treated when I were in that house for three years. (2023)

When I came here first, when I said about my journey and my story, I thought nobody can trust me or listen to me. But the first time I saw [ICTG worker], he understood my problem. He tried to help. ... And ... it have [sic] been done successfully and everybody persuaded about my story, they everybody understand [sic] and I have been believed in the end. (2023)

I just wanted to say [ICTG worker] has been helping me since they took me out of the prison, and he came here every week, talked to me and spent a lot of time with me to help me. He's like a family member. He's been helping me a lot. (2023)

Young people compared advocates and independent guardians to brothers, fathers or parents on occasions. Likewise, the support of less formal advocates, in the absence of an ICTG presence, were also described as being like family:

OK, family, I am not living with my family now. My family is [name of organisation] [laughter]. Because, of course, they are people who do not understand, now I come here and are telling them some problem, [name of organisation] is doing everything, like some problem with the hospital ... it is important. (2022)

There was a level of trust shown and belief towards ICTGs and other advocates and, for young people, having someone they could trust became a specific outcome statement in the ICTG service study. This outcomes statement on 'I have people I can trust who support me' was as a result of support from their Barnardo's worker. Trust was closely connected to the relationship young people had with their ICTG:

> You know, before I met you, I never trusted anybody at all. Because the experience that I went through being exploited and being used. So, I never believe that anyone would help me but after meeting you, you made me feel that I can trust in you. I could talk to you. I could confide in you and all that because of the support that you gave me and have been giving me. (2023)

And, for some, their ICTG was the *only* person they could trust:

> OK, I do trust Barnardo's. They're very honest. I do trust them. And [ICTG worker], because he's the one working with me. Apart from you, I don't trust anybody else. (2023)

> OK, I have been good supported while I was working with [ICTG worker] because whenever I have … had a problem. … I felt like he was helping me, understanding me and believing me, but the other support workers are not the same. … I don't feel I have a good relationship between me and them. I don't. I don't think they believe me and myself, I don't trust them. … When I was with [ICTG support worker], always the day was ending with very laughing and the happiness all the time. But, with them, it's always not ended with this kind of emotion. (2023)

It was also clear from discussions in the CSF study workshops that young people valued having someone who could stand by them and advocate for their best interests:

> They [ICTGs] make sure you get a good lawyer; they choose a lawyer for you and they come to the lawyer

with you and make sure you get a good interpreter because they've got experience with interpreters. ... And Guardians had other people before us, so they got a long experience and even worked in other places before in this kind of area. So, they got a lot of experience with different interpreters, and they know which one. And also, lawyers, which is very important as well. (2022)

Similarly, all 25 young people engaged in the second study felt supported by their ICTGs and considered them instrumental to their participation, protection, and achievement of positive outcomes:

He trusts. He has got a big trust on [ICTG worker] because she's honest and always stands with him. (2023)

Young people in the ICTG service study also considered their Guardians as important in helping them to understand and navigate the complex systems they found themselves in and to communicate with the multiple professionals involved in their lives, as one ICTG narrated to a young person they were supporting:

I can imagine that it was really difficult at the beginning because you had a lot of professionals working with you and a lot of people you didn't know, and you didn't understand what their roles were. And after everything that you've been through, I imagine it was very difficult to trust people in general, right? (2023)

Having people to trust also meant young people were able to develop safe friendships:

Many young people [come here] and we are doing many activities that I didn't do, and we are doing here at [name of organisation] and we meet many people, and staff and other young people that we have got many friends here. (2022)

> You can make ... friends. That's how I made my friends ... through a *safe* [speaker emphasis] network, yeah. ... See, when I met friends in Guardianship, like you know where they're all coming from and you know who is taking care of them and you know that these people are safe, in a safe accommodation, taken care of and not doing anything. (2022)

> So, basically, they helped me with find more friends because I did not really have any friends when I came here, and Barnardo's helps me to meet other people, and I feel less lonely because of that. (2023)

In turn, young people gained self-confidence, learning many unwritten rules about their new environments and the related systems and processes:

> She tells me in detail what's happening and what's gonna happen next and if it's a good one and it's a bad one. So, she explains in detail about it, and I always get confused about things because I don't know anything here. So, I had to ask her to understand everything. (2023)

As can be seen, the approach adopted by ICTGs or informal advocates in areas where they were present made a difference for young people. Having someone to turn to, who they trusted, who kept them up to date, who would stand by them when they needed it and help them find safe relationships and friendships was beneficial. In comparison to the attitudes and practices of other professionals outlined in Chapter 3 and how this impacted on the relationships built, the ICTG service can be seen here as changing practice in relation to children and young people affected by human trafficking, including around discrimination, equality and best interests of the child. ICTGs being able to act as such 'trusted adults' was a key finding of the MS Outcomes study.

'I feel cared for'

Few studies focus on protective factors in the lives of children and young people affected by human trafficking or exploitation. The literature reviewed as part of the CSF study on human trafficking overwhelmingly focused on risk factors and negative outcomes, including negative health outcomes as well as a range of negative consequences stemming out of exploitation. However, protective factors can include having positive self-esteem, hope, spirituality, doing well at school and following interests (Radford et al, 2020). As already seen, relationships based on trust, that are supportive, provide good emotional support and good peer relationships can also protect children. Having social connections, access to good quality care, rights to legal protection and access to supportive adults are known protective factors at a wider level. There is already clear evidence available that shows how children who have experienced sexual exploitation who 'do not blame themselves and have someone to confide in have fewer adverse consequences' (Radford et al, 2020: 56). Tapping into, and talking about, this range of protective factors was part of this, with young people outlining how, in their view, their best interests were met, including feeling cared for:

> When someone cares about you, basically they care for your wellbeing, they care about like your thoughts, probably your situation, what you're going through and stuff like that, so when someone is showing you care … (2022)

For young people in the CSF study, having a 'good' independent guardian, 'good' social worker or 'good' solicitor was related to whether they felt cared for and were subsequently able to navigate services. Having professionals show them empathy was also part of this:

> They show you sympathy, empathy, because they are actually trying to feel what you are feeling at that point, so because the best way for you to help someone, you have to put yourself in that position to actually support the person. (2022)

> Yeah, I agree with that position, because if you are receiving good care from your foster carers or from friends and, you know, when you care for others as well, you're happy, good care is really important for young people. (2022)

Other young people engaged in the research on the ICTG service spoke about being or feeling cared for as a result of support from their ICTGs, both in relation to accessing services and 'practical' care – 'I eat, I dress well, I'm safe, I'm in a home' (2023) – but also being emotionally cared for including being treated with kindness and not feeling alone:

> Everyone been helping me really well and I feel safe, and my needs are met. Everyone is really kind and care for me. (2023)

Most of the young people engaged in this research connected feeling cared for with how they were treated and looked after by their ICTG, sometimes comparing this feeling of closeness and emotional care to that of having a family member or friend: 'I felt that I had a friend and that she came often to support me' (2023).

'I can have my family with me' or 'I can have safe contact with my family if I want to'

In the past few decades, there has been increasing awareness that family life can be the basis of nurturing and growth for children or, alternatively, a place where abuse and violence can be regularly experienced or witnessed. There has also been a growing recognition that child protection responses have focused on younger children and on inside the family home, and that risks of maltreatment and abuse for older children often occur outside the home (Firmin, 2017). 'Contextual safeguarding' as an approach introduces risks outside the family home and these less recognised extra-familial harms challenge the existing child protection system to include a broader age group, different locations in which harm can occur, and different forms of harm. Contextual safeguarding, therefore, makes space for ensuring the safety of young people as well as younger children and, in doing so, has questioned 'systems and beliefs that have allowed adolescents to be criminalised, blamed and made responsible for their abuse' (Wroe and Manister, 2024: 1).

For young people in both studies included in this book, abuse and exploitation could have taken place inside or outside the family home, potentially en route to, or once within the UK. Young people may arrive without a figure of parental responsibility in their lives, but it is not the absence of family per se, rather the absence of family in the UK, that places them in need of protection. Forms in which harm may have occurred could be multiple, encompassing physical, emotional and sexual abuse as well as neglect in UK child protection terms. Certainly, as recounted in Chapter 3, many young people felt unsupported and not always cared for by systems and processes in the UK. For these young people, questions around family – and family reunification – are complicated, as one young person outlined:

> We start by saying every child and young person needs protection. … One of the main things is protection of your family, which not every person has the luxury of a family, or their protection. And there is other young people who *need protection from their family* [speaker emphasis]. That is a totally different thing. (2022)

In the CSF study, an outcome emerged around their wanting to have family with them in the future – 'I can have my family with me'. This invokes the need for many to go through – or intend to go through – further complicated legal procedures in the UK. Such family reunification was on the mind of many young people who openly discussed barriers to this process. The creation of families in the future also emerged as part of the aspirations and dreams of young people to feel loved, welcomed, in control of their own lives, and to create and feel a sense of belonging.

In the MS Outcomes study, the outcome statement utilised was amended to 'I can have safe contact with my family if I want to', invoking on one occasion a request to an ICTG not to speak about family during meetings:

> Can I ask a question? I want to ask what is the reason, for every meeting, I have been asked about my own family and has been all the time being asked? What is the reason for that? (2023)

The ICTG worker responded that they wanted to ensure the young person's family were well and that they also wanted to ensure the young person was not worried about them. For this young person, having to recall and speak about their family caused upset and stress:

> So, that just gives me tension that every time my family has been asked in the meeting. I say I don't have, or I don't know, or something, but this gives me a reminder of my family and for two to three days after the meeting, I still think about the time I had with my family and the worries come back. So, I would really like not to be asked, OK? (2023)

For many young people in both studies, the absence of family *in the UK* caused this type of stress. Within the MS Outcomes study, however, the cohort included some young people supported by the ICTG service who were from the UK and who had no contact with their family, despite their being present in the UK, for other reasons.

This complex positioning of young people in relation to their families and their own protection, as well as expectation of engaging both UK-born and non-UK-born young people in the research, prompted the second study's use of 'I can have safe contact with my family if I want to'. This outcome statement aimed to also relate to where young people's family histories were part of the reason for their journeys, which could be potentially harmful for them or their families in some way. There are various scenarios of why this might occur. As Leon and Rosen (2023) detail, complex relationships around debt and indebtedness to support transnational families or support peers are complex but relate closely to the ways young people create their own forms of social protection despite hostile policies being enacted towards them. Chase and Allsopp (2021) explain the transnational nature of young people's relationships, including the way in which persecution from within their families may necessitate cutting off all contact with family members 'as a strategy of survival and self-protection' (2021: 192–3).

Across all young people, different situations within families were involved – too many to recount here. It was, however, of note that a focus on family environments played out in discussions around those who were supporting and advocating for them in informal or formal ways.

Conclusion

It is clear from the empirical material provided in this chapter that the principle of best interests as contained in Article 3 of the UNCRC was understood by young people in both studies. In the CSF study, it was repeatedly stated that gaining legal status meant young people could move forward with their lives and the importance of accessing high quality legal advice and gaining legal status cannot be understated. However, the years of waiting and being pulled back into telling and retelling their accounts to different professionals involved were repeatedly recounted as being sources of stress and distress. During this time young people needed to be kept informed about the status of their application, know who to turn to for help, and who to contact for the information they needed. However, we question whether leaving young people waiting for their legal status and documentation while repeatedly requiring them to recount their (often traumatic) histories could ever be in their best interests.

Although the published literature on human trafficking focuses overwhelmingly on the negative outcomes and consequences of exploitation, young people in both studies discussed positive outcomes they felt were in their best interests. Guardians were especially good at engaging with young people and bringing them a sense of feeling cared for, regaining a sense of wellbeing and helping young people navigate the constrained environments in which they were living with a sustained focus on best interests throughout. They were also a touchstone for a young person's sense of safety and protection which we will consider in Chapter 5, as well as their unfolding social, emotional and physical development in this context.

FIVE

The search for safety and restoring everyday life

Introduction

We have been living in many different places. (2022)

Yes, so when you are in transit, you don't feel safe. (2022)

In my opinion the most reason you come here because … their countries, they don't have safe life. Everybody have different problem, but I see most of them, this is their problem, because they don't have safe life in their background. (2022)

If you don't trust, you don't ask for protection. (2022)

Yes, I feel very supported, and I feel very confident, since I arrived here, I was only 14 years old and during … this time the support that I have received, I have gained confidence, I have and been supported with the accommodation financially … and passport status. … Everything I have, so now I'm getting older. (2023)

Article 6 of the United Nations Convention on the Rights of the Child (UNCRC), on the right to life, survival and development, places an obligation on governments to ensure that children are protected from violence, abuse and exploitation, and that governments do all they can for children to survive and develop to their full potential. This chapter draws on further empirical material generated in both the CSF and MS Outcomes studies to explore this obligation. As with previous chapters, it forefronts the views of young people, providing first-hand accounts of how this principle is understood as well as experienced in practice.

This chapter considers Article 6 in three distinct ways. First, we consider safety – safety to ensure not only the right to life element of the UNCRC, but as a foundation stone for the realisation of other rights and outcomes and involving a young person both being safe and feeling safe. We already have insight into what Richmond (1994) and others since (Chase, 2013) have outlined in terms of how a person's 'primary ontological security' can be threatened or taken away when needing to leave family, communities and countries of origin (Richmond, 1994: 19). This feeling of being 'in transit' and the need to find such a sense of ontological security in everyday routines, so as to restore a 'degree of predictability and trust in others' (Richmond, 1994: 19) and regain self-confidence, came through from young people's accounts:

> Safety, yeah, is very important. Like, you must have experienced something that is so difficult. And when we come here because we still feel that panic, you know, that trauma. (2022)

An ongoing search for safety runs through these accounts and here we consider aspects of physical, relational and psychological safety. As we have detailed in previous chapters, this search for safety is politically charged for this population of young people.

Second, we consider the need for protection – protection not only for survival, but protection from abuse, harm and any future exploitation. Young people had a broad conception of what protection meant to them; this is explored, including other protective factors that may be transnational in nature and based on relationships that stretch across the geographies of their lives.

Third, we take note of the lack of evidence on how experiences of human trafficking affect the physical, emotional and social development of this population of young people. From recognising this knowledge gap, we move towards understanding what young people themselves considered they needed for their development to be healthy and meaningful in their lives.

This chapter therefore begins by looking at safety, followed by the broad conception of protection as understood by young people in both studies. Thereafter, a brief overview of factors related to the relevant stage of adolescence in terms of child development is provided and related to their rights under Article 6. Within this, we explore the agency of young people and their ability to achieve, to obtain desired education, to have a viable future, to be healthy and, simply, to have fun and enjoy life surrounded by friends and supportive adults.

'I am safe' and 'I feel safe'

Safety emerged as a fundamental priority for young people engaged in both studies and was considered as foundational for the realisation of their other rights and entitlements. However, as outlined at the start of this chapter, young people discussed not feeling safe, 'living in different places' and being 'in transit' prior to their arrival into the UK and then having to actively search for safety once here. Two clear and specific outcomes emerged from the CSF study, with young people identifying both 'I am safe' and 'I feel safe' as complementary and desired outcomes for their lives. In the MS Outcomes study, two aspects of safety – being safe as well as the avoidance of harms – were prioritised by young people and the ICTG workers supporting them, leading to the outcome statement 'I am safe and protected from harm', explored further here in the section on protection.

When discussing the practicalities underpinning safety, young people tended first to detail basic needs and support, in order to feel shielded and protected. Other basic needs outlined included access to education, employment (or other stage-appropriate responsibilities), medical services, feeling as though they could grow into being an adult with confidence and without fear, having friends around them, and access to familiar food. The search for safety was thus multifaceted and we elaborate here on its physical, relational and psychological dimensions.

Physical safety

Key to discussions about safety was the physical security of having age or stage-appropriate accommodation:

> The house. ... Like, accommodation, to give you a sense of protection, a sense of safety. (2022)

> I feel protected. I feel I've been looked after ... in terms of giving me this accommodation. (2023)

Other basic needs being met within the accommodation provided made it feel safer:

> I eat. I dress well. I'm safe. I'm in a home. (2023)

> That means that you're, you get, like, plenty of food. You can use the bathroom and have a shower. You've got a comfortable bed. (2023)

However, it was not always the case that young people felt safe in the accommodation that was allocated to them:

> She's not in a good place right now. (2023)

Young people not only spoke about a sense of safety in their own accommodation but also that of their friends under the age of 18. In the CSF study, discussion around the outcome 'I am safe' also included young people no longer being sought by those who had exploited them and feeling safe from future exploitation, and living in safe communities was part of this. Children also discussed being able to sleep safely in their accommodation.

Relational safety

Beyond the physical security provided, there was an expressed need for people who could help them – who, it was reiterated, needed always to be 'nice and kind'. Such staff could help them, show them how to shop, cook and feel supported:

> Then we go back there to home and she started to cook with me, and she tried to chat with me, and then she said and she do a lot of things to make you laugh, you know, something like that. Because she tried – I understand why – because she tried to get me the mood where I come from to be, like, comfortable and then I start my life, you know, like that. (2022)

A sense of physical safety was deepened by young people having support structures like these around them, including trusting relationships with friends and professionals, in what felt like safe communities. The distinction between 'safe' and 'unsafe' friendships was apparent:

> In my case, for me when I go to college, something I've experienced a lot, there's always type of that friendship,

people that always … you feel like if I follow these people, I'm not safe, the language, the body language as well … so I feel like it's really important to know who you are working with, what you do out there, anything that can make you feel safe is very important for young people, put ourselves first before we get, like, say … somebody [who] can help us feel safe. (2022)

Making friends could be complex for those living for the first time in the UK:

If you are new in the country, like, you haven't got any friend. For me it was a bit hard because, like, I have no friend, and I was, like, little bit struggling at school. (2023)

Friendships made during this period, through professionals who understood the risks they had faced or were facing, were crucial:

See, when I met friends in Guardianship, like you know where they're all coming from and you know who is taking care of them and you know that these people are safe, in a safe accommodation, taken care of and not doing anything. (2022)

Opportunities to make new friends could come from organisations advocating for young people but other young people had made friends independently:

So, at the house that I was at previously, there were lots of people there. Ten of us, all together so there was no need for anyone to help me to make friends because there were friends there. And then when I went to college, lots of people there who I made friends with. (2023)

Some young people had not had good experiences of making new friends. For example, one young person had shared personal information with others she met on arrival, and they had gone on to tell others:

> And when you first come, you think like they [friends] are like your family, you treat them as your family. ... And that's a very important thing I would say to all young people: don't share all your information with anyone, even if you feel miserable, even if you feel like you want to talk with someone and you feel like you're exploding to share your emotions or your sadness or what you went through, because they're going to use it against you no matter what. (2022)

Reference to potential vulnerability within community settings was mentioned but, as one young person outlined, advice from their ICTG had prompted an awareness of relational safety:

> I think safety ... for myself, it depends on who you follow, what you do and who you do it with. So, I feel, like, before you really talk about safety, make sure you yourself feel safe and you avoid bad stuff, and have good friends, people around you. Make sure you follow the right things ... (2022)

Living in communities that felt safe fed into this sense of relational safety:

> I feel, like, as a new person in a new country you basically don't know how the country works or how the system works, so you don't know anything, you don't know anyone in the country, you're new or even if you know someone in the country, you technically don't have an idea, so community first, like, it needs to be safe ... (2022)

Trust in professionals and having other people to trust around them and provide emotional support was key, and reiterated throughout:

> ... having people that you trust around you and having people who tell you who to trust and not trust. (2022)

In the MS Outcomes study, ICTGs were highlighted as trusted adults providing such a sense of relational safety:

> Yeah, so ever since I met you, you started working with me. I felt safe. I felt that I'm protected. (2023)

> I do feel safe from the job that [ICTG worker], you, sir, and the others around you have done throughout, because initially you made me feel safe, then made me open up and talk about my fears and what I was worried about. And that is why this has turned out ok. (2023)

Linked to this was the role of foster carers, advocates, personal advisers and others supporting young people within accommodation.

Psychological safety

Psychological safety for young people, expressed as 'I feel safe', meant being able to sleep safely in their accommodation, that this accommodation was appropriate to their age, and that they knew where to go and who to turn to when they did not feel safe. Good quality care and knowledge about their immediate community was also important. For example, being able to sleep in allocated accommodation was directly related to young people's past trauma:

> The staff need to be kind and nice because maybe people are coming from traumatic experiences. Staff have to be very understanding of what we have been through. (2022)

And safe house as well is very important for people to feel safe when they're sleeping or whatever, because when you come in a new country, even if something small moves, you feel like, 'Oh, my God, something happening', or, 'Something, someone coming to my door', and you don't know. (2022)

It is important for people to feel safe when they are sleeping in a new country. (2022)

Likewise, knowing where to go when they did not feel safe and knowing who to trust and turn to was central to this feeling of psychological safety:

They will need [to] make them feel like again, 'I'm here for you, here you can speak to me when you feel unsafe' ... it's just about the worry in you all the time, so it's really important for that. (2022)

Trust, credibility and commitment in relationships between children and professionals sat at the heart of this sense of safety, especially in relation to creating psychologically safe spaces for potential disclosures and subsequent better identification of exploitation to occur. This type of psychological safety was as important as physical safety to young people, who identified the potential of police and interpreters in immigration and care procedures to play a meaningful role in creating psychological security for them:

We fear the police because they are so brutal. ... We had mentoring on how the police here and back home are different. ... Who are they protecting against? Like drugs, criminal gangs ... we fear child abuse, statelessness. (2022)

With young people you need to be more friendly. The same way they have special interpreters for the NHS, they [the Home Office] should be that way. (2022)

A default response of disbelief from professionals, already mentioned in Chapter 3, undermined this psychological safety, making young people feel frightened and unsafe:

> I don't feel I have a good relationship between me and them. I don't. I don't think they believe me and myself, I don't trust them. … When I was with [ICTG], always the day was end[ed] with very laughing and the happiness all the time. But with them is always not ended with this kind of emotion. (2023)

Accounts of exploitation – of friends or others within their networks – were only ever a few steps away for those without secure legal status:

> I spoke to a friend yesterday and she told me she was working for some organisation, maybe like a restaurant, because they were like … if you work for like 12 hours, then they pay you for just six hours … [and] instead of giving you your full amount for that six hours, they split it … they give you the pay for three hours this month, three hours next month. … And that's for not having papers. (2022)

One of the outcomes that emerged from the CSF study was 'I know my rights and entitlements'. A key part of this for young people in both studies was awareness of their rights in the UK, as well as having access to rights-based organisations increasing their feeling of security:

> [Organisations are] giving your rights and everything like that … so you feel safe. (2022)

> She tell me you have rights. If, umm, you want to do this or if you don't want to, you have right as well to refuse. (2023)

These three interrelated elements of safety – physical, relational and psychological – were linked to protection in the views of young people, explored in the next section.

Protection of children and young people: 'I am safe and protected from harm'

Internationally, Bhabha (2008, 2014, 2016) has identified how the international legal framework impinges on children who migrate and how there is an untold and unanalysed narrative to their complex backstories. Outlining how approaches adopted within international and domestic law differ, Bhabha has described how approaches can be 'punitive and criminalizing', 'regulatory' or 'protective' (2008: 1, 2014). Whereas it might be assumed that a protective approach would be proffered to all children and young people with lived experience of human trafficking, worldwide this is not always the case. Children can be criminalised and penalised with regulatory approaches which establish legal parameters for the migration of children and which often assume 'children are dependents of the family unit, without autonomous agency' (Bhabha, 2016: 6). Whereas the vulnerabilities of children have been a key focus, requiring protective policies and legislation, Bhabha suggests that *equally necessary* is the *agency* of children and the opportunity to be heard. We explore this further in Chapter 6.

However, for children forcibly migrating to the UK, protection can also refer to a more international form of protection. This is protection as it relates to a child fleeing persecution or the fear of persecution and seeking protection from the UK, as a nation-state and signatory to the 1951 Refugee Convention. Importantly, for children who are trafficked, the 2000 Palermo Protocol does not require states to support victims of trafficking through the same long-term protection as for refugees.

Young people who have lived experience of human trafficking in the UK are not automatically approached through a protective lens. Bovarnick (2010), for example, noted definitional pluralism, a polarisation of opinion between 'immigration-centred' and 'child-centred' discourse, when trafficking was a relatively new field of practice. Bovarnick also found that trafficking was challenging localised knowledge and safeguarding practices in the UK, with limited awareness in practice alongside the duty to safeguard. As detailed in Chapter 3, discriminatory and immigration-centred practice still occurs, and, as in Chapter 4, there remains an ongoing tension between what the state and young people consider to be in their best interests.

Protection is a fundamental element of children's right to life, survival and development. The severity of and length of time over which abuse takes place affect adverse outcomes, but consequences do vary. Part of this variance relates to protective factors, such as the individual child's resilience and inner resources, their interpretation of experiences they have had, the strength of family relationships, availability of emotional support, friendships, spirituality and sense of community. In other words, children's and young people's place in the world, their self-esteem and access to support when needed is key. This particular mix of potential vulnerabilities and resilience of each young person requires consideration.

Firmin's 'contextual safeguarding' has brought a contextual lens that has 'resulted in children, whose lives are in danger, sitting beyond the parameters of the systems designed to protect them from harm' (2020: 250). Areas of child protection referred to here relate to adolescents, families and broader communities past child protection systems did not reach, beyond the home environment where 'extra-familial harms' occur (Firmin, 2020).

For children and young people with lived experience of human trafficking a focus on such extra-familial harms is essential. Contextual safeguarding focuses on the situations children and young people might find themselves in, something embodied by the very definition of human trafficking – an abuse of a position of vulnerability. Safeguarding as 'everybody's responsibility' then should extend to children and young people in exploitative situations. A firmly child-centred rather than immigration-centred discourse in relation to all forms of abuse associated with and experienced amid human trafficking is required.

Young people engaged in our two research studies had a broad conception of what protection meant for them. Protection took on a range of meanings and was understood in different ways. This included protection as 'safety' as already detailed. It also included protection as faith, belief, trust, confidence, the rule of law, knowing their rights and entitlements, access to education, safe accommodation, and friendships.

Young people referred to protection from harm and abuse, from external actors:

> I'm feeling safe and protected from the horrible things. ... Horrible things that you know the people do to you. (2023)

They also described actively 'fighting' to find, build and achieve protection for themselves:

> I just feel like this story stands out to me because of, you know, he worked hard to get protection, which is like similar to what everyone's going through ... because we need these papers to stay and get protection from this country ... it's part of the process, it's part of fighting. (2022)

> Even it's now, regardless of your situation, if you are working towards some project as well, staying part of it and just working hard to achieve something, so the achievement at the end of the day is protection. (2022)

Young people reflected on how they had had to draw on their personal histories and what they had been through as part of this fight to find and enhance their protection:

That's because of what you said, you said your history becomes your protection, so I think it's a bit kind of deep, so knowing that what I've been through in the past, I've fought to – because I got to stay in this country and get my stay. (2022)

We had to leave where we are from to come to this country … leaving that protection … and now you need to use what you've got, to get protection for yourself. (2022)

During these discussions, distinctions between themselves and 'British children' featured, with young people born outside the UK reflecting on protections afforded by legal status as a form of shield:

They are born with protection: so, it is just like you having your father in the house having a British passport. (2022)

I was thinking about people, you know, like, if you are British, you have a British passport and … that means you are bringing out a shield that is definitely automatically protected. (2022)

For another young person, with both secure accommodation and status to remain in the UK, he was finally feeling protected and safe:

I feel protected. I feel I've been looked after, been given opportunities, been looked after in terms of giving me this accommodation. Yeah, you know, and, also, I feel safe and protected because this country has given me authority to stay here. (2023)

For others, this protection felt potentially quite transitory:

... and it can be revoked back from the court, knowing that if you do anything silly or any mistake, it will be revoked and it would be taken back from you. (2022)

Gaining protection for many young people was then part of a 'journey' they saw themselves on.

Young people in both studies described protective spaces, such as within the education system, and how these enhanced a sense of protection in broader terms:

Education as well. ... Yeah, I feel like where you're studying, you feel like your future is being protected. (2022)

Yeah, I mean they, they let me to have education and talk a lot about safety and just very protective and prevent. (2023)

Beyond education, young people talked about protection relating to a range of services providing for their basic needs, accessing safety and support through different routes as well as supportive networks, including professionals:

You lost the first protection back home with your family, everyone else around you that feel protected like that, but then you just come back to this country and see a lot of people, like your foster carer ... then they start making your protection. (2022)

Young people also discussed different protective 'layers' (for example, friends, family and trusted adults). For some young people, these trusted adults were also considered 'family':

I agree with him regarding family could be not just blood and I think when you came here, I think, I remember when I was with my family, there's no difference between [name of organisation] and my family. (2022)

Finally, young people spoke about their *own* ability to protect themselves and strategies they employed to do this in the absence of protective family members:

> See, another thing that people will mainly use it against you is when you tell them that you don't have family. They'll feel like you have no protection. ... I never tell people that I don't have family. I always say, 'I've got relatives around that support me', or ... I'll say, 'Yeah, I've got relatives, I've got cousins, I've got people who support me and help me', and I just don't give any other information, like tell them, 'Oh, no, I live alone', or, 'I don't have anyone', or stuff like this. (2022)

Agency demonstrated by young people to find, fight for and ultimately achieve protection became clear during these studies. Reflections on their personal histories and pasts was part of this. To do this, young people drew on their strengths, capabilities and endurance of the often-protracted processes they found themselves in.

Child development

There is a lack of evidence on how human trafficking affects the physical, emotional and social development of young people, partly because literature on children's social development and children's rights have evolved separately (Bhabha, 2014; Lott et al, 2023; Todres and Kilkelly, 2025). For young people affected by human trafficking, child development – and its various stages – is not reflected in law and policy which cuts across a range of ages, nationalities (including the UK), and types of exploitation.

Different theories and approaches have been used to make sense of child development: for example, Erikson's (1979) eight stages of psychosocial development where children's personalities evolve as social relationships and interactions affect their development and growth.

Socio-ecological models, emerging out of child development and child maltreatment studies, place the child at the centre and relate this to their surrounding environment (Bronfenbrenner, 1979; further developed by Belsky, 1993). These have been applied to a range of social issues including child sexual exploitation and abuse (Radford et al, 2015 a,b; Radford et al, 2020) and have led to contextual safeguarding approaches (Barter, 2009; Firmin, 2020). Zimmerman et al (2015) have applied socio-ecological thinking to the human trafficking of adults, suggesting it allows for larger contextual forces to be considered alongside individual factors.

Frameworks have been built on ecological approaches advocating for a public health approach to child protection, for example, the *Framework for the Assessment of Children in Need and their Families* (Department of Health, 2000) or 'assessment triangle'. This encourages a broader approach to child protection, with the child at the centre, having three key components: the child's developmental needs, family and environmental factors, and parenting capacity. However, this framework does not encompass work across borders (Hurley et al, 2015).

What is important here is understanding that child development is a process potentially requiring language and stage/age-appropriate responses for physical, cognitive, spiritual, psychological and social potential to be fully reached.

Adolescence is often seen as a stage of particular risk or a time that might lead to poor outcomes for young people due to their specific situations. This period has been seen as an ambiguous time between being a child and adult. However, as Huegler (2021) outlines, the construction of adolescence as a 'life phase' has changed significantly over the past two decades. This is based on evidence from serious case reviews, thematic reviews and specific inquiries, suggesting that this phase may last from early teenage years to late twenties (an age range of 10- to 25-years-old). Huegler outlines how this development is influenced: 'Significantly, adolescent development is influenced by complex intersections between social inequality and the impact of adverse experiences and trauma throughout childhood and adolescence' (Huegler, 2021: 4). The child protection system's lack of focus on risks and harms outside the family home for these young people and the adult safeguarding lack of emphasis on young people are both detailed as lacking (Huegler, 2021: 5). These risks include different forms of exploitation, including child sexual exploitation (CSE) and child criminal exploitation (CCE) for UK-born children. In this book, these forms also necessarily include labour exploitation, domestic servitude and other forms, each occurring outside the family home and, often, with the absence of a figure of parental responsibility within the UK.

Other Articles within the UNCRC relating to the right to education and health are relevant here and young people in both studies spoke about outcomes related to these.

The significance of education: 'I can access education, achieve and have dreams'

In Chapter 3, we explored the significance of young people not being able to access education. This was due to informal and formal exclusions in law and practice around eligibility and a hierarchy of rights based around legal status. Access to education, training and stage-appropriate employment opportunities were a mixed challenge for young people in the CSF study. For example, those with 'refugee' status were fully eligible for student finance and paid 'home' rates for university entry, whereas for 'unaccompanied asylum-seeking children' (also commonly referred to as UASC), those with 'discretionary leave' or 'limited leave' to remain in the UK, this was more difficult:

> Asylum-seekers, they can't go to university [but] they can study part-time in college. This one needs to change as well, because they want to study and they might get

papers a year later, which is they're just wasting a year and wasting some modules ... it's not fair just because you're waiting for an answer you can't do full-time course, or you can't go to uni. (2022)

As outlined earlier in this book, this need to wait to undertake what other young people were able to begin at age-appropriate times was considered an additional and unequal burden for these young people. Access to education was considered as giving young people the ability to understand UK systems and processes:

When you first come here, school or education, they're going to learn about the system of the UK and they're going to know about what they have to do and what the government have to do so they know their rights. (2022)

English for speakers of other languages (ESOL) classes were also much discussed, with some young people suggesting these should be combined with vocational training and others wanting opportunities like apprenticeships.

'I am healthy'

Discussing access to health services revealed a mixed picture. Some young people in the CSF study could not register easily with GPs, get appointments or were having to wait, creating upset and stress:

The GPs are really nice and important in our life and they help. But only one thing, for example, if I book appointment for the GPs, I have to wait longer and then I go, they give me like another appointment and that other appointment – you hear me? – takes very longer. And that is the real pain I have here. (2022)

They don't even answer my phone. I've been checking for an appointment for a year now and then I didn't go. (2022)

Organisations supporting young people sometimes accompanied them to these appointments or, in a few cases, took them to walk-in clinics, considered more accessible and useful.

In the MS Outcomes study young people responded to the statement 'my body and mind are healthy' in relation to ICTG service support. For some this was about getting access to health services:

> I have told ... the worker about my health issue and what makes me worried about my health ... for example, my skin on my face ... so, I don't know what has the worker done, whether they have spoken with others or they have tried to get me support ... (2023)

For others, it was about support to feel healthy through access to activities and sport: 'I go to football' (2023) and 'I do lot of gym' (2023) and 'just to go out, talk about things ... have a little, like, walk' (2023). This access to fresh air and activity contrasted with their previous exploitative and confined situations. For one young person, due to ICTG service support, he had been able to 'move out and live more comfortably, have fresh air', life was now 'wonderful' and he was feeling 'healthier day by day' (2023).

For another, this support had improved his health considerably:

> I used to stay in the home most of the time. Sometimes I go, like, to the coffee shop, but after they [the ICTG service] got involved in my life, I start going to other places ... I have new ideas and new people that's ... had a positive impact on my life ... I feel better, so that's affected my habits. Now I eat much better than before because I feel good. (2023)

Others provided examples of how their relationship with their ICTG worker had enabled them to access counselling, feel emotionally supported or be more at peace.

'I have a stable life' and 'I feel calm and in control of my life'

Young people in the CSF study emphasised a sense of self-actualisation and being able to find purpose in their lives, wanting a stable life in which they could have and achieve dreams as part of confident, stable and safe futures. Young people also wanted opportunities to succeed:

> [They need to be given] the opportunity to achieve what they are good at. (2022)

> Even if that person doesn't have their document, you know the person's really good at this thing, he's got opportunity, that is an opportunity to actually add value to the community or to the country, so you have to give them the opportunity to actually do that what they are good at. (2022)

Young people in the MS Outcomes study responded positively to the statement 'I feel calm and in control of my life', with most feeling calmer than before ICTG service support:

> Because I had a lot of things going wrong in my head on my mind and [therapist] helped me an awful lot. (2023)

> So, I was in this place, a very bad place, for a very long time. Three years and when [ICTG worker] started working with me, he made me feel calm. He took me out. He talked to me, he listened to me. That was very important. That he listened to me and believed in me and that made me feel as if I am important. (2023)

Having a trusted relationship with their ICTG worker has meant these young people feel supported, less fearful and more confident about their lives: 'At college, looking forward to future, feeling in control' (2023).

Young people in the MS Outcomes study also mostly agreed with the statement 'I have hope and can plan for a better future'. Examples included: 'housing and Home Office and future and staying in the UK' (2023), and joining a cricket academy: 'you know, for the future' (2023).

Young people also detailed how their own background influenced their decisions in this search for an everyday, stable and positive future. This need to feel calm and in control and being able to move forward was a key finding for young people across both studies.

'I am able to have fun and enjoy myself'

Young people spoke about opportunities provided to have fun and enjoy themselves:

> Happiness is ... having the opportunity to do what you love. (2022)

In the MS Outcomes study, young people shared examples of when they had been 'taken out' by their ICTG worker – to a garden, a park, to go shopping or for for a walk – but also supported them to do something that they really wanted to do:

> I remember I [was] really keen on joining a football team and she work really, really hard to get me enrolled in this [name of football club]. For me to play football and it was really good. I remember feeling wonderful. (2023)

Such opportunities to have fun closely connected with young people's sense of improved physical and mental health as well as with their identity, culture and religion, since activities included accessing places of worship, buying items of cultural and religious significance, and eating culturally appropriate food:

I get to know how to buy stuff in the shops because when I came is very important for young people when they first come to know where to buy food. ... They want food from their country. (2022)

Conclusion

It is clear from the empirical material provided in this chapter that the right to life, survival and development as contained in Article 6 of the UNCRC was an area of considerable interest and concern for young people. Their safety, right to life and survival demanded protective spaces be found and young people worked hard to achieve this. Beyond mere survival, the right to develop in various facets of their lives was, where possible, being fully embraced. The right to fulfil these developmental aspects were, in other cases, restrained by administrative categories and legal classifications.

Overall, this chapter outlines young people's perspectives and reflects on why this right to life, survival and development emerged as the most discussed UNCRC Article in the CSF study. Young people in CSF workshops drew on their personal histories and original motivations for migration to find the strength to pursue an active search for safety and protection in the UK. Young survivors connected to and spoke about their own strengths and capabilities while simultaneously drawing on their capacity to endure complex and often protracted social care, immigration, and criminal justice processes in the UK.

These findings are comparable to those from the MS Outcomes study, where young people articulated the multiple positive outcomes for them and their lives from having ICTG service support. Despite exclusions faced, young survivors reflected positively on their current situation as well on their hopes and aspirations for the future. These young people focused more on the 'here and now' of their present situations which, with all but one young person, was presented as more positive and preferrable to their past. This illustrates, we suggest, the positive role of having the ICTG service to support them, help them navigate complex and often politicised processes, and move through the blend of care and control around them.

SIX

Child participation and agency

Introduction

I am not here to eat, drink and sleep. (Young person at the Parliamentary launch of Creating Stable Futures Positive Outcomes Framework)

But the Home Office, sometimes they listen and sometimes they don't or sometimes they just decide whatever they want to do. So, like we don't have the power to do there. So, they have all the right to do whatever they want to do. (2022)

I've just felt so much listened to. I think it was so nice that you [ICTG worker] were prepared to listen to me. And when I first came here, I was not familiar with the environment, with the way that the family lived here. And you were helping me, explaining everything to me. And you were always there, listening to my concerns and helping me and making sure that I understand everything. (2023)

> Thank you – you heard me when no one was listening. (Young person, quoted in ICTG service case-closure summary)

These quotations tell us much about how young people affected by human trafficking want to participate in matters affecting them and in society more broadly. Young people involved in our two studies told us about being listened to in some cases and contexts, but not in others and welcomed taking part in our two research studies.

The participation of children and young people in matters impacting them is embodied by Article 12 of the United Nations Convention on the Rights of the Child (UNCRC). This Article states that every child has a right to express their views, feelings and wishes in all matters affecting them, and to have these views considered and taken seriously, in accordance with their age and maturity. This universal right to participation applies to all children at all times and in all spaces, including, for example, during immigration and judicial proceedings as well as decisions around accommodation, access to health services and education. In addition, as noted in Chapter 1, Article 12 is an instrumental right, enabling children to access their other rights under the Convention.

Despite this, participation has been repeatedly identified as a particular weakness in the international evidence-base relating to children's rights, which includes evidence on the human trafficking of children and young people. Within this evidence, it is not always clear if the views of children are included beyond being participants in individual qualitative studies (Batomen Kuimi et al, 2018; Ibrahim et al, 2019; Albright et al, 2020; Malhorta and Elnakib, 2021). This is also the case where studies include both children and adults (Hemmings et al, 2016; Cannon et al, 2018; Cockbain et al, 2018; Okech et al, 2018; Simkhada et al, 2018; Dell et al, 2019; Graham et al, 2019; Garg et al, 2020; Such et al, 2020; Knight et al, 2022). Knight et al (2022) specifically detail a lack of participatory methods and recommend that future research should be culturally and contextually relevant to those affected. Within this literature, however, there are suggestions that child protection systems do have mechanisms for children's participation in safeguarding policy and services (see, for example, Radford et al, 2020).

In submissions to the CSF study global call for evidence, children's views are also rarely requested by or included in the literature about them, even for those studies pertaining to children's rights. That both the international literature review *and* the global call for evidence find children's views are rarely elicited or included in research about them including on their rights, is striking.

This supports Bhabha's (2008) contention that the right to participation has not featured as prominently as the other three General Principles considered in this book, meaning that the 'voice' and subsequent 'influence' of children and young people has been heard less than that of the professionals working with them:

> This perspective has been virtually non-existent in the evolution of the legal framework governing child migration, where denial of the child migrant's capacity for autonomous agency has been the guiding principle. Independent child migrants, as a matter of law, have generally been regarded as suspect, either passive victims of exploitation ... or undeserving illegals ... or adults masquerading as children. (Bhabha, 2008: 2)

Bhabha outlines how, when this right to participation is applied to child migration, it brings a new dimension which acknowledges the capabilities and agency of young people and has potential to influence policy and legislation. Such potential for new insights is also true of children's participation in human trafficking research, a process which can occupy ambiguous spaces but could also lead to new narratives. Beyond being one of children's inalienable *rights*, a substantial bank of literature, as noted in Chapter 1, evidences the *benefits* of children's participation for their protection, including for children and young people who are forced to migrate.

There are caveats with this approach, including for children struggling against discrimination and fighting for equal rights. Participation is differently defined with, for example, Hart's (1992) 'ladder' of child participation a reflection on the differing degrees of children's 'voice' in matters that affect them, ranging from 'non-participation' with 'manipulation by adults' as the lowest rung to 'child-initiated, shared decisions with adults' as the highest. In both our studies, funding was sought by adults and then an ethos of co-production was fostered, placing them on the 'adult-initiated, shared decisions with children' rung of Hart's ladder. However, even research designs fully positioned at the top of this ladder may encounter limitations in terms of impact, if the political space and political will, commitment to improve children's lives and resources or funding are not available.

This chapter provides first-hand accounts from young people affected by human trafficking on their participation and how this principle of participation is experienced and seen as being reflected in policy and practice. Through this, we shed light on how a non-tokenistic and more meaningful form of participation of children and young people affected by human trafficking in research and practice can be further supported and framed (see also the section on key learning in Chapter 2).

In both the Creating Stable Futures and MS Outcome studies, young people affected by human trafficking emphasised the importance of being listened to, having what they said matter in decisions made about them, understanding others and, in turn, being understood. Issues around trust and mistrust and healthy relationships with trusted adults again emerged as important, closely connected to a sense of being listened to, heard and believed. At a broader scale, young people in the first study explored how, ultimately, they would be contributing to society in the longer term. In the second study, some young people were at a stage where they were less able to consider or envision this. These themes now form the basis of this chapter and, given the UK's obligations under the UNCRC as well as domestic law around child protection, should be given what Lundy (2007) refers to as due 'audience' and 'influence' in legislation, policy and practice relating to young survivors of human trafficking.

'I am listened to and what I say matters'

In both the Creating Stable Futures and MS Outcomes studies, young people responded well to their thoughts, views, needs, hopes and aspirations being encouraged and voiced during workshops and Q-sorts with the researchers. Young people participating spoke about how they did or did not feel listened to and whether they thought what they said mattered to practitioners and others around them.

In the CSF study, being listened to, respected and having what they said, thought, felt and wanted matter to those working alongside them was a message running through young people's accounts. This 'voice' was, however, contingent on feeling safe and comfortable to speak:

> Because when you feel comfortable, as you said, so you would be more open and will speak. Because the voice is the most heavy element to demonstrate what you want, so, like, you have to be adapt and feel comfortable around, so then you can speak up. (2022)

For another young person, this was associated with the approach teachers, social workers and other professionals needed to take for young people to feel listened to and seen as a person, not a 'client' or a 'case':

> Just treat them as a friend, like as a new friend coming to a new country. How would you treat if someone came to your family? And how would you feel, the city, the

food, how would you try to explain? And that would work out. (2022)

This was reiterated in the MS Outcomes study, with one young person distinguishing between being 'listened to' by their foster carer and being truly heard:

> I have been listened to. ... I have said my problems and things I need to say so I don't feel, don't know whether that has been accepted, whether it, say, matters to them or not, but I have been listened to. (2023)

In the MS Outcomes study, it was almost always the ICTG that the young person feels has enabled them to be more fully engaged:

> You were the only one, from the beginning, who really talked to me. (2023)

Young people participating in the CSF study similarly spoke positively about being listened to and supported by their Guardians, if they lived in areas where they had access to ICTGs:

> But they're really supporting you. Same like here with the Guardianship or something, you know, in your daily life, you arrive, and even if you have appointments, you know, or college, everything you know, they help you. (2022)

For these young people, it was important that they were also seeing results, that their 'voice' was being conveyed further and influencing others:

> When I needed some things, like, I can contact her. She can tell to my social worker or my PA, [personal adviser] she has helped me with that couple of time, and my lawyers, yeah. (2023)

It was felt that ICTGs were also essential in conveying their 'voice' further, into areas where any connection or influence over policy could feel out of their reach, as fore-fronted in this chapter, but also relayed by other young people:

> We speak to our Guardianship and our Guardianship speak to our lawyers. Yeah, from then they will, but then Home Office is going to hear our voice. (2022)

This potential for wider influence was also important during their participation in the research:

> I'm sure that all this information that you two guys [have] will be passed [to] people where they need to know about this. (2022)

> And I think this is a good opportunity. We share our voices with you … without you we can't share our voices … we don't know how [we] can send our voices to like a government or Home Office or any other direction. (2022)

For others, without access to ICTGs, there was some frustration at not being heard:

> Or sometimes you just have to speak more, yeah, because I think the Home Office are people that needs to hear your voice multiple times. You know … because you don't have to be just quiet and waiting for the decision because you have to speak your mind and let them know that how you're feeling is really depressing. So, you have to speak more for them to understand what you're going through. (2022)

It was clear that young people enjoyed participating with others in these studies:

I don't know how to say it but through the eyes I can [tell] that you are listening to me. … Well, yes, you know something but for myself I feel it by heart and I just saw through your eyes that you see things. (2022)

I meet new people and they were nice, and I learn a lot in this group. (2022)

Yes, so it's comfortable for me to say, it's, say my, say out loud my experience. And you are listening to me and that made me feel. … It's like I feel nice because when I say something, someone listen. Not like I talk to the wall. (2022)

The group is really, really important. Get to express what you know and to learn what you don't know. … And from there I feel comfortable like speaking because I like to express myself in many, many things, what I'm facing, you know? So, the group gave me the courage to build up this my centre to explore. (2022)

The sense that 'voice' alone was not enough was restated by a young person, who felt that they had had 'space' to talk but that the 'audience' and 'influence' to affect 'government or Home Office' policy was out of their reach:

And I think this is a good opportunity. We share our voices with you … without you we can't share our voices … we don't know how [we] can send our voices to like a government or Home Office or any other direction. That why's I thank you, thank you guys for coming here and nice to be here with you. … And also, I thank all the group. They did work hard, and they shared their own information and this, from their kindness to help other young people to get, like, a best life or best, to get, like, their right or something like that, or they have, like, a little bit change for their difficulties. Yeah, thank you very much. (2022)

Or that it was too late to influence their situation but there could be improvement for others in the future, as another young person who had been through the process of gaining legal status detailed:

> It's not going to change anything [for] me because I think I've passed that kind of stage for myself. I'm done with the Home Office, I'm done with the support. ... But it will be great that other persons, they don't go through the same difficulties that I was through, make it easier for them. ... So, if that helps anyone in any ways I will be very happy and that's why, that's the reason that I've participated as well. (2022)

Across both the CSF and MS Outcomes studies, Lundy's model permeated the approach adopted and the preoccupations of the young people involved. This process of being truly listened to also related to accessing help to communicate if they needed it and being understood and able to understand others.

'I am understood and understand others'

Within the CSF study this outcome related to the ways in which young people could access materials in their own language and dialect and, for one young person, meeting someone who spoke the same dialect was key:

> For me, I met my first couple of friends in college. So, I didn't have anyone who speaks my language where I was living, so I just met them in college, so it helped me a lot. (2022)

Other reflections on this outcome related to well-trained interpreters and the need for young people to have their cultural and religious needs provided for and respected. It was also connected by young people to professionals understanding the impact of immigration procedures on young people's wellbeing and understanding the processes they were involved in and the decisions being made about their lives.

In the MS Outcomes study, this outcome statement was developed into 'I understand what's happening to me and what others are telling me'. This study showed how young people felt supported by their ICTG worker to understand what was happening to them and, in turn, to be understood. For example:

> I mean, she tells me in details what's happening and what's gonna happen next and if it's a good one [or] it's bad one. So, she explains in details about it, and I always get confused about things because I don't know anything here, so I had to ask her to understand everything, so that's why. (2023)

Similarly, as an ICTG worker detailed:

> So, I think what I, what I understand is that this young person understands what is happening to him, in terms of maybe like social services or immigration and all the systems that this young person is involved in. So, I think it's more about that. (2023)

Overall, it was clear across both studies that the need to understand and be understood was vital for young people so that they could effectively navigate the systems and processes they found themselves in, as well as feel connected to others around them.

'I am trusted' and 'I have people I can trust to support me'

The need to feel trusted and be able to trust others ran through our discussions with young people. Some relayed how they might have been betrayed during their journeys but also in the situations they found themselves in. As one young person powerfully recounted:

> From the question one to the last one, it's all about trust ... trust is the most important thing. People don't give easily. So, like, it's difficult for me to trust right now here because what I've been through is a lot ... you know? People I was not even expecting stab my back ... it's difficult for me to earn that trust right now because I feel guilty if I'm going to have it ... yeah, because I don't want my heart to be cut again, you know? So, trust is the most important thing in all of this discussion. (2022)

This relates to the sense of ontological security and safety already detailed in Chapter 5:

> And because, why I'm talking this, because when I came here ... you know, because I have a problem and I have a hard life until I get here, so [this is] why I don't trust anyone, because I'm thinking, 'Do I have right to stay here?', and, 'Can I be safe here?', you know. (2022)

Young people were also clear that working with professionals they trusted changed their worlds and was central to their protection and relational safety:

> Yeah, so ever since I met you, you started working with me, I felt safe. I felt that I'm protected and that I have a voice. (2023)

> Trust, trust is 100 per cent very important. I trust with her so much, I would share any problem with her and she would support me with that and give me advice. (2022)

The success of social policies often rests on a fulcrum of trust, wherein those affected by policy regard this as helpful to them:

> And it's also something maybe, what you're saying, that we could ask from other professionals that, 'If you want me to get better or to feel protected or to open up, I need this trust and if you want me to trust you, I also need to trust, yeah?'. (2022)

In relation to this trust, the ICTG service and its Independent Guardians were again considered instrumental:

> 'The Guardian I think is really important for young people ... they have like special experience with young people. Even the way they talk to the young people ... that's really, really important and really special. They listen to the young people and they give you advice and they help you if you have any problem or if you need any help, they are able to help you at any time. For example, now I'm not under Guardianship care anymore but I think now if I have a big problem, I'll contact with my Guardianship firstly and my social worker. Yeah, so it's very important. (2022)

Building trust with children and young people is one of five ICTG service aims and central to the independent guardianship of children: 'We meet children face-to-face to build trusted relationships to support them through the complex systems and processes they find themselves in.' Trust is highlighted by young people engaged in the MS Outcomes study as a key contributing factor to the positive outcomes they connect with ICTG service support. For some, their ICTG worker was the *only* person they felt that they could trust.

It's clear from the research that this trust is built on how the ICTG worker relates to the young person, listening and acting on what is said, consistently and reliably over time:

Yes. So ... when I first came to this house, I was so lonely, and you came, and you befriended me, and you were so kind and caring. And you took me out and you introduced me to other people, and I made friends ... all thanks to you. And you were always there for me. You made me feel not lonely anymore. (2023)

Trust for young people in the MS Outcomes study was also closely related to feeling believed. This might be belief in them from their foster carers or families:

Yeah, I feel very much believed. And I believe them, because, otherwise, if there is no belief, then how would a family that I don't know anything about it, would they trust me, let me stay there and then leave me living in their house, and then ... how can I live my life with a family who I never knew? So, it's all about the belief in them, the trust. So yeah, I agree with that. (2023)

Or it might come from the ICTG workers supporting them:

I believe in me because for all this length of time that I have been supported and whenever I have problem issue, I speak to them and they listen to me and they are so many meetings. So obviously this should prove that they believe in me to listen to me, to give me meeting and all the time that I have been here. If they wouldn't have believed me, I wouldn't be here. (2023)

In some cases, it is the ICTG worker alone who believes the young person:

OK, if I, if I want to talk about being ... believed ... or being heard, my voice being heard here, the first when I came here, nobody listened to my story, or the ones who listened to my story being very, I refused and not believed. Just the first time when I met [ICTG worker], he was the only one who understand my problem. He was, have a good understanding and good support and he believed me. He helped me to get here. (2023)

A default response of disbelief was also experienced by young people in the CSF study, making them feel frightened and unsafe. Trust was also related to circumstances wherein young people did not trust family members, or many others, but could see pathways towards trusting relationships one day:

… like, you can't find it [sense of family] somewhere else unless you create your own family and have your own children. (2022)

'I can contribute to society'

In the CSF study's workshops, young people outlined how, despite often having uncertain and ambiguous legal status, they wanted to contribute to society:

Another one is independence and help to society as well. (2022)

Even if that person doesn't have their document, you know the person's really good at this thing, he's got opportunity, that is an opportunity to actually add value to the community or to the country, so you have to give them the opportunity to actually do that what they are good at. (2022)

In the MS Outcomes study, some young people were more unsure about whether they could contribute to their community at this point in their recovery and in their lives:

> I can't do something to help my community. Like, I don't feel like there is anything that I can do right now. Maybe in future, but, like what [the ICTG service is] giving me, it's about me right now, they're not focusing about something I can do for others. Right now, what I feel, it's more focused on my health and my happiness on my side and things like that. (2023)

> At the moment, I'm not in a good position to help the community because I haven't been settled yet, but in the future, when I, everything is good, when fine with me, I'm happy. I'm ready to have the community if they want help, but at the moment, as you said, it's not in my field. (2023)

For others, supporting the community was something that everyone could do:

> Obviously everyone wants to help, to be helpful in, in the community, but I have not had anyone asking me to help me with this, that I would say whether I'm able to help that person in the community or not, but we all, we all try to help. (2023)

> Well, you could. You would tell someone to come, come, to me. Just like I really want to help her, doesn't matter who, Muslim, non-Muslim, in the sake of humanity. Humanity – we are all human and all human lives to be helpful to each other. (2023)

> Like helping other people here anywhere, college, mosque, in the house, in the community. (2023)

Some young people talked about how they were helped by their ICTGs to engage with and integrate more in their local community, making friends and helping others as a result:

> Yeah, you help me to, to, to meet other people, to have a spare time on Saturday and also to get involved with sport activities. (2023)

> Yes. So, you know, it's so obvious, because of you. You've taken me to introduce me to other friends, to other Vietnamese people ... because of you that I've got friends, that I feel less lonely. So, you know, the fact that we are together as a group, we're helping each other. (2023)

One interpreter also commented about another young person:

> [ICTG worker] showed him some youth club and he used to go, even yesterday he been there and that's really helpful and communicat[ing] with people, and he likes it. (2023)

It was clear from the research that young people were at different stages and had different needs and perspectives as a result, which the ICTG service worked flexibly to support.

Conclusion

Both of these participatory studies had a focus on child rights and the importance of children's participation as it related to their protection. Both spent time ensuring a safe space for young people affected by human trafficking to give their views and be heard through policy and practice-related research. The particular mix of care and control through policies enacted meant that many of the young people in these studies were living with uncertain and ambiguous legal status and limitations on their participation in matters affecting them. This is important against a background where the views of children affected by human trafficking, modern slavery and/or exploitation have been rarely requested or included in the literature about them and supports a stance which welcomes a young 'survivor turn' in the field of modern slavery, centring the participation of these children and young people and their views.

Both studies put young people at the centre and both studies revealed how such an approach resulted in young people proffering solutions, which are explored in the next chapter (Chapter 7). The two studies combined found that there is a lack of focus on longer-term outcomes for children and young people post-trafficking or post-exploitation. It was also found that pathways towards positive outcomes are contingent on ensuring work with children and young people is participatory, child-centred, and has a rights and entitlements approach, that is underpinned by relational approaches built on trust. There is considerable need for further participation of young people, not only to hear their 'voices', but so they have the right to be heard, with policy makers as their audience so they can inform and influence policy and make this fit for practice.

We suggest that taking this type of participation seriously could ultimately mean the human trafficking sector in the UK could better understand not only the lives of young people, but also the ways in which a focus on positive outcomes in their post-trafficking lives could contribute to ensuring their and others' recovery and wellbeing. This positive side is a relatively unexplored aspect of human trafficking, but is essential if young people are to move forward with their lives. In Chapter 7 we detail an unanticipated but welcome and much needed development towards the end of the CSF study – the creation of a Positive Outcomes Framework for survivors of human trafficking – which went on to inform the MS Outcomes study.

SEVEN

Development and implementation of a Positive Outcomes Framework

Introduction

For children and young people affected by human trafficking, modern slavery and/or exploitation, there is very little focus on post-trafficking outcomes within existing literature and, where this exists, considerable variance on what is meant by the term 'outcomes' (see Chapter 2). For those wanting to move forward with their lives, there is a distinct lack of focus on necessary post-trafficking outcomes and, across the small number of studies considering this, few accounts that reflect on or include the needs, capabilities or aspirations of these children and young people.

Both the CSF and MS Outcomes research studies sought to address this gap in understanding through participatory research. Much qualitative research is preoccupied with researchers seeing through the eyes of people involved (Bryman, 2012). Participatory research positions people as the experts of their own experience, accepting knowledge can be generated in this way, while also allowing for power dynamics during research to be addressed, colonial legacies to be recognised as well as broader structural inequalities involved that go beyond the reach of any one individual (Hart, 2008).

As discussed in Chapter 6, Hart's (1992) 'ladder' of child participation reflects on the differing degrees of children's 'voice' in matters that affect them, ranging from the lower 'rungs' of non-participation to the higher which are child-initiated and directed. Rung 6 is 'adult-initiated, shared decisions with children' which, given funding mechanisms for research, is where most research projects with children are situated including the two studies focused on in this book.

Literature reviewed for the CSF study identified a range of outcomes, but no pre-determined outcomes were introduced prior to or during the workshops with young people to ensure their views were prioritised. An emphasis on the process of research – as a process of possibility – allowed young people to reflect on their lives, the procedures and services that they had experienced to date. A key aspect of this process was to allow young people the time and freedom to be able to create, reflect, connect with their peers and the research team. This was not about young people relaying their experiences of trafficking, but about hearing what works in service provision and where improvements could be made aligned with their own priorities. Similarly, while the MS Outcomes study identified an initial 'concourse' of outcome statements, including those drawn from the Creating Stable Futures Positive Outcomes Framework (CSF-POF), for use by young people in assessing the ICTG service, the Young People's Advisory Group advised on those most relevant, accessible and appropriate and shaped the final statement selection.

Participatory research is by nature an unpredictable process, involves occupying ambiguous spaces, and can lead to unexpected findings. A key principle or benefit is that those closest to the problem being addressed often have key insight into the best solutions. Working alongside and with those who have lived experience not only of human trafficking, but also of subsequent service provision, means listening and hearing about priorities that may be different to those anticipated, for example, beyond existing or predominant narratives built up within disparate policy, legislation and services.

This chapter details an unanticipated but welcome and much needed development towards the end of the CSF study – the creation of a full Positive Outcomes Framework for young survivors of human trafficking with 25 distinct 'outcomes' and 86 associated 'indicators', grouped around the four General Principles of the United Nations Convention on the Rights of the Child (UNCRC). It recounts the development of this CSF-POF and the way in which this was employed by the MS Outcomes study for an analysis of the ICTG service. Reflections on adaptations in practice and some conclusions complete this chapter.

Development of a Creating Stable Futures Positive Outcomes Framework

The workshops with young people for the CSF study described in Chapter 2 had, as part of identifying important outcomes, young people being invited to think about the relationship between their needs and the positive differences that could be made through support and interventions that were in their best interests. This process of exploration involved encouraging young people to reflect on outcomes more generally and a holistic array of outcomes were identified as a result.

The surfacing of these 25 distinct outcomes is the first time we know what young people identify as outcomes that are important and meaningful to them, represented through their words and in first person statements. They represent what young people identified they would need in place for positive and meaningful changes to happen in their lives and the lives of others, now and in the future. An additional 86 associated 'indicators' were identified from this same process to allow elaboration of what each outcome would mean in practice. Ultimately these outcomes made up the CSF-POF (see Figure 7.1).

Figure 7.1: Creating a Stable Futures Positive Outcomes Framework

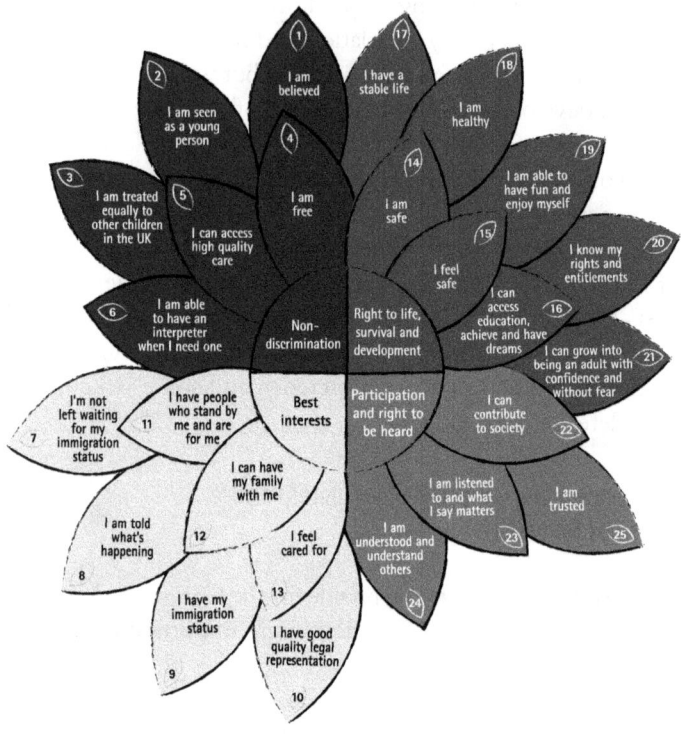

Source: Hynes, Connolly and Duran (2022)

A key strength in this process lay with the mixed academic and voluntary sector team, which allowed for cross-fertilisation of ideas. Each outcome and indicator were written in the first person, directly from quotes in transcripts. After the development of the outcomes and indicators in this way, a 'wrap up' participation workshop was held with young people in each location to give feedback on their generous input and verify the final results and content of the framework.

As can be seen, the four General Principles of the UNCRC sit at the centre of this tool, with the 25 individual outcome statements surrounding them. The full list of 25 outcomes and 86 associated indicators is detailed in Table 7.1.

Table 7.1: Table of CSF-POF outcomes and indicators

	Outcome	Indicators
1.	I am believed	– Children report their age is accepted unless there is a significant reason not to – Children report their account of exploitation is believed
2.	I am seen as a young person	– Children say they are not expected to fend for themselves – Children report they are given appropriate independence – Children say they are treated as children first
3.	I am treated equally to other children in the UK	– Children say their treatment from professionals such as policy and social workers is equal – Children report not being blamed for decisions made by adults
4.	I am free	– Children report they are not afraid of being exploited again – Children report they can enjoy their rights without fear
5.	I can access high quality care	– People working for the services around children are well trained – People working for the services around children understand where they are coming from – People working with children are friendly and respectful – Children say professionals work together – Children report their privacy is respected – Children know how they can complain if there is a problem
6.	I am able to have an interpreter when I need one	– Children say interpreters speak their language and dialect – Interpreters are well trained – Interpreters are child-friendly – Children are asked if they are comfortable with the interpreter

(continued)

Table 7.1: Table of CSF-POF outcomes and indicators (continued)

	Outcome	Indicators
7.	I am not left waiting for my immigration status	– Children are given clear information about the immigration process in child-friendly ways – Children report receiving timely decisions
8.	I am told what's happening	– Children report knowing where to find information and who to contact for help – Children report they received sufficient communication from officials regarding the status of their application – Children are appointed an independent legal guardian
9.	I have my immigration status	– Children receive a decision which is based on their best interests as the primary consideration
10.	I have good quality legal representation	– Children receive advice from a solicitor who can represent them appropriately in complex legal situations – Children can access solicitors who understand trauma
11.	I have people who stand by me and are for me	– Children have foster carers and support workers who understand their needs – Children say they have someone who takes responsibility for checking in and making sure they are OK – Children say they have access to independent advocates or guardians
12.	I can have my family with me	– Children report feeling able to create a family in the future – Children state they feel protected from their family if they pose a risk of harm – Children can access procedures for family reunion without due burden
13.	I feel cared for	– Children report feeling cared for – Children report not feeling alone

Table 7.1: Table of CSF-POF outcomes and indicators (continued)

	Outcome	Indicators
14.	I am safe	– Children report not being sought by the people who trafficked them – Children report not being afraid about debts – Children and young people report feeling safe from future exploitation
		– Children and their families are protected from harm – Children say they live in safe communities – Children say they have trusting relationships that protect them – Children say professionals understand the risk they have or are facing
15.	I feel safe	– Children report being able to sleep safely in their accommodation – Children say their accommodation is appropriate to their age – Children report knowing where to go when they don't feel safe and who to turn to – Children receive quality care – Children say they are informed about the communities they live in
16.	I can access education, achieve and have dreams	– Children can attend school promptly – Children report having access to additional educational support if needed – Children say their talents are known and supported to grow – Young people can attend college or university – Young people can undertake vocational training and ESOL simultaneously – Young people can uptake apprenticeships or other employment opportunities – Young people report being able to concentrate on their studies – Young people say they can move on from their experiences in positive ways – Children report they have confidence in their future

(continued)

Table 7.1: Table of CSF-POF outcomes and indicators (continued)

	Outcome	Indicators
17.	I have a stable life	– Children report they can begin to recover from their experiences – Children say they can plan for their future and make decisions – Children say they feel at peace
18.	I am healthy	– Children are promptly registered with a GP – Children have access to appropriate mental health services – Children can access specialist medical advice – Young people report they can access the food they enjoy
19.	I am able to have fun and enjoy myself	– Children report they can play and participate in sports – Children have access to leisure and entertainment activities – Children and young people report they are able to form healthy friendships
20.	I know my rights and entitlements	– Children report they have support to learn about their rights and entitlements – Children say their rights are upheld and they can access their entitlements
21.	I can grow into being an adult with confidence and without fear	– Children report they are not afraid of approaching age 18 and have been supported for this – Children say they feel confident they will be supported when they turn 18 – Children report they are able to do stage-appropriate activities – Children report they are able to take on stage-appropriate responsibilities
22.	I can contribute to society	– Young people report feeling they are able to 'give' to society

Table 7.1: Table of CSF-POF outcomes and indicators (continued)

	Outcome	Indicators
23.	I am listened to and what I say matters	– Children report feeling they are being listened to and respected – Children can access help to communicate if they need it – Children report being asked what they think, feel and want – Children are included in research about them – Children report being asked their thoughts and listed to in the development of policy that affects them
24.	I am understood and understand others	– Children can access appropriate materials in their own language and dialect – Children can get a trained interpreter when they need one – Children report their cultural and religious needs are provided for and respected – Professionals working with children understand the impact immigration procedures have on their wellbeing – Children say they are asked if they understand the processes they are involved in – Children say they are asked if they understand the decisions that are made about their lives
25.	I am trusted	– Children report feeling trusted – Children report they can trust professionals

Of these 25 outcomes, two would not be applicable to UK-born children and young people and a further two may not be applicable. Outcomes 7 and 9 that relate directly to immigration status will not be relevant. Outcomes 6 and 12 about the use of interpreters and related to family members may not be applicable. This leaves 21 outcomes that are potentially significant when working with UK-born children.

The CSF-POF is intended to be a holistic tool and can be used in many ways:

- at an individual level, as an empowerment tool when working with young people who have been affected by exploitation and are wanting to move forward with their lives;
- for frontline workers in social care, social justice and/or immigration to allow them to 'tune in' to the needs and experiences of young people during conversations;
- as a harm prevention tool when discussing risks and future potential harms with children and young people;
- when conducting assessments, recording the wishes of children and young people in care, pathway planning, advocacy and support work when discussing referrals into the National Referral Mechanism (NRM);
- by local authority children's services in case audit reviews to determine if children are achieving positive outcomes post-trafficking; and
- at a policy level, to determine the potential or impact of specific policy initiatives.

Overall, use of the outcomes devised by children and young people could mean that the efforts of those working with them will be focused on creating stable and positive futures.

Implementation of the CSF-POF: outcomes for children and young people affected by modern slavery

Chapter 2 set out how a participatory methodology called Q-methodology was employed by the MS Outcomes study with young people affected by human trafficking to explore outcomes for them from ICTG service support. This research drew on the CSF-POF, building on and adapting the ethos and framing of the 25 positive aspirational outcomes co-developed with young survivors for a more child-centred approach: that is, one built on outcomes generated by and that matter to children and young people themselves.

This analysis of the ICTG service represents the first implementation of the CSF-POF with young people in practice, used as part of a service evaluation. A brief outline of the process followed provides us with an account of the adaptations made and the rationale for those changes, plus space for reflection and learning.

Q-methodology, to enable the exploration of different perspectives and priorities, requires an initial 'concourse' of possible evidence-based statements to be set out. All statements are worded in response to a central 'provocation', which, in the case of this study, was 'Because of support from my Barnardo's worker ...', situating young people's responses within the context of outcomes related to ICTG service support. Adaptations to the 25 outcomes reflected this practice-facing context.

The 'concourse' of statements developed drew on the 25 outcome statements from the CSF-POF (see Table 7.1) as well as other sources, including, for example, the ICTG service aims and associated outcome areas and the cost-of-living crisis. The adaptations also included evidence relating to outcomes for UK-born children and young people affected by human trafficking, reflecting the study's aim to engage both UK-born and non-UK-born 'young people' over the age of 11 years old. An initial set of 34 statements was explored, piloted and co-adapted with the study's Young People's Advisory Group (YPAG), all with lived experience of human trafficking, and through review by a small group of ICTG service practitioners and relevant experts to get a final 'Q-set' of 28 statements for the research. The resulting 'Q-set' of 28 statements for the study on the ICTG service in response to the initial provocation were:

'Because of support from my Barnardo's worker...'

1. ... what I say is believed
2. ... people treat me similarly to other young people my age
3. ... my culture, religion and identity are respected
4. ... my experiences and needs are understood

5. ... I can make choices that are important to me
6. ... I am involved in decisions made about me
7. ... I am well cared for and my needs are met
8. ... I can get support to communicate with others
9. ... important decisions about my life are made quickly
10. ... people do what's best for me
11. ... I have people I can trust who support me
12. ... I can have safe contact with my family if I want to
13. ... I have friends that are good for me
14. ... I feel able to care for others
15. ... I do not feel alone
16. ... I am safe and protected from harm
17. ... the risks I face are understood
18. ... I can achieve things
19. ... I can have the education I need
20. ... I have hope and can plan for a better future
21. ... I feel calm and in control of my life
22. ... my body and mind are healthy
23. ... I am able to have fun and enjoy myself
24. ... I know my rights and what support I should have
25. ... I feel supported and more confident about getting older
26. ... I can do something to help my community
27. ... I am listened to and what I say matters
28. ... I understand what's happening to me and what others are telling me

In practice, Q-sorts were conducted using these 28 statements with 25 young people between the ages of 15–18 who were being or had been supported by the ICTG service, only two of whom were UK-born. Reflections from young people on these outcome statements in relation to ICTG service support included:

- Wanting an example or more explanation on some of the statements or just not understanding the terms used. For example: 'I can get support to communicate with others',

A POSITIVE OUTCOMES FRAMEWORK

both UK- and non-UK-born young people wanted to know what kind of support; 'my experiences and needs are understood', some did not understand what was meant by 'experiences' but most understood 'needs'. Under 'the risks I face are understood', some young people were not clear what these risks were.

- Understanding the statements differently to anticipated. For example: understanding 'important decisions about my life are made quickly' to be a bad thing, signifying that not enough attention was being given to the decision or that the decision would not be the best for them, whereas in the CSF-POF being 'left waiting' for decisions on immigration status was not positive.
- Conversely, quickly grasping the meaning of some of the statements and wanting to elaborate and tell their stories. For example: in relation to the outcome statement 'my culture, religion and identity are respected', young people spoke easily about instances of such respect and support from their ICTG workers; for the statement 'I have people I can trust to support me', most young people mentioned their ICTG worker as a trusted adult.
- Putting statements to one side or not commenting on them during the Q-sort because they did not want to discuss them. For example: the statement 'I can have safe contact with my family if I want to' was clearly sensitive for some young people.
- Suggesting statements that in future could be added to the Q-set, including one outcome statement related to increased self-confidence and another related to improved financial and/or material wellbeing.

These reflections are important and demonstrate young people's agency and influence on the statements through the Q-sort activity and in the MS Outcomes study where they can still question, disregard or make suggestions and have meaningful participation.

Reflections from ICTGs on the outcome statements, including those engaged at an earlier stage in their development but also after supporting their use in the Q-sorts with young people, were also insightful. These included:

- The importance of a strong focus on children and young people's participation – not as 'passengers' but active in their own protection through the ICTG service. Statements on being involved in decisions, making choices, being listened to, understanding and being understood were all important to reinforce this emphasis in the service.
- The statement 'I can have safe contact with my family if I want to' being too sensitive or difficult for some young people to touch on. This was demonstrated by a support worker helping the young person to put this to one side or supporting this not being discussed in the Q-sort.
- System- and status-related decisions being important outcomes for young people supported by the service and impacting upon them and their wellbeing in multiple ways, even if young people did not specifically talk about these systems and processes in connection with the statements shared.
- Concern about some statements, for example, 'I feel able to care for others' and 'I can do something to help my community', as somehow a requirement for young people and their recovery and the sense that these young people just being able to care for and help themselves is enough.

This research on the ICTG service engaged young people communicating through several languages, including Kurdish Sorani, Pashto, Tigre, Arabic, Albanian, French, and Vietnamese, supported by interpreters and with the set of outcome statements translated into these different languages. Six out of 25 young people participated in the Q-sort in English. For two of the study's statements, the interpreter mistranslated and the young people concerned were confused.

For example, in Vietnamese, the statement 'I can achieve things' (statement 18) was mistranslated as 'I can achieve everything', which the young people concerned initially disagreed with until the interpretation was corrected. In addition, 'I feel supported and more confident about getting older' (statement 25) was mistranslated in Vietnamese as 'getting old'.

Barrow et al (2021) use Q-methodology to explore what is valued by young people and frontline staff from child sexual exploitation (CSE) services. While the findings have some similarities and relevance to the CSF and Outcomes for Children and Young People Affected by Modern Slavery studies (as mentioned in Chapter 2), the young people engaged take a less participatory role in the development and amendment of the Q-set of statements, which appear to be solely developed by the authors and an adult practitioner 'expert by experience'. Statements are initially drawn from the extant literature on CSE, but there is no mention of whether any of these are based on the opinions, priorities and views of young survivors of CSE.

Piddington et al (2024) have commented on research by Robyn (2004) translating a Q-set originally in French into seven different European languages, and the challenges of establishing equivalence through this approach. Indeed, meaning and understanding are fluid, influenced by language, culture and context, and direct translations are not always possible. Here the research is being conducted across multiple national contexts rather than solely in the UK, as for this study, although the young people engaged have multiple countries of origin and languages of choice.

It is important to note that while the young people engaged in the CSF study co-developed the POF outcome statements through multiple sessions over a year, the young people engaged in the MS Outcomes study (as the YPAG in developing the Q-set) engaged with and responded to a set of outcome statements only once. What this meant in practice was that they did not have the same background, context or shared, nuanced understanding of the statements and so were likely to have more amendments and suggested edits to make their own sense of them as a result. For the CSF-POF going forward, however, children and young people may similarly need to respond, react to and potentially also rank the 25 outcome statements without this background. The further piloting of the CSF-POF and its 25 statements is already underway across the UK, with practitioners testing its use with children and young people of different ages, abilities and those who are UK-born. This will help us know what works across the diversity of children and young people with lived experience of human trafficking and exploitation.

Conclusion

Chapters 3 to 6 focused on the four General Principles of the UNCRC and how these are experienced and negotiated in practice in the lives of young people affected by human trafficking engaged in both the CSF and MS Outcomes studies. The contributions and views of these young people build and gain momentum across the four chapters to address the gap in evidence, in UK and international literature and in policy identified at the beginning of this book. Young people's words also make the case for a deliberate, rights-based and holistic focus on positive, post-trafficking outcomes for children and young people.

This chapter has outlined the development of a framework for driving and enabling such a paradigm shift – the CSF-POF – and has provided an account of its first implementation in a participatory service evaluation with young survivors of human trafficking and the learning involved. We now reflect on the previous chapters, bringing these different threads together into concluding remarks and, in doing so, identify new insights and new directions from these two child-centred research studies.

EIGHT

Conclusions, new insights and new directions from child-centred research

At the beginning of this book, we set out to address a significant evidence gap in relation to positive, post-trafficking outcomes for children and young people affected by human trafficking in the UK. We also sought to detail how young people related to their rights under the UNCRC and how this led to the development of a positive outcomes framework which was then implemented within the ICTG service. Throughout, we foregrounded their views and have raised questions about the positioning of these children and young people, based on their participation in our research. This positioning relates to, and has provided us with new insights on, among others, the shifting landscape of terminology connected with human trafficking, modern slavery and exploitation; the relationship between exploitation, child safeguarding and protection; and the need for better support for children during transitions to adult services.

This contribution to academic, policy and practice debates on positive post-trafficking outcomes involved two participatory research studies. Both took the participation of children seriously, with research as a process of possibility, so that the views, knowledge and experience of children and young people could be placed at the centre.

While it is recognised in the UK that the human trafficking and exploitation of children is first and foremost child abuse, as we have seen in previous chapters, this premise does not always reach policy, interventions and practice. This chapter outlines how responses to children and young people affected by human trafficking and exploitation now need to be firmly rooted in child welfare and child rights approaches rather than viewed through criminalising or immigration lenses (Bovarnick, 2010; Wroe, 2021; Lloyd et al, 2023). We have also reflected on changes in the child protection and safeguarding landscape, from a focus on younger children and harms within the family home towards a more inclusive perspective involving older children and risks outside the home (Firmin, 2020). For children or young people with lived experience of exploitation, the former model does not fit well with the protection challenges they face of extra-familial risks from within and beyond the UK.

This contribution

The ethical participation of children and young people in research takes time, and collaboration with partners already working with these young people proved especially constructive. Making research processes inviting and welcoming, with young people listened to and believed, can result in a sense of unspoken reciprocity and, as we found, valuable and relevant insights emerge.

Looking through the lens of non-discrimination, we found a gap between this principle and practice. The negative impacts of immigration procedures and routine barriers to full inclusion were felt by young people, affecting their everyday encounters with professionals. These were in part mitigated in areas with an ICTG service and/or other frontline practitioners advocating for them – that 'one person' who would stand by them and guide them through often complex and protracted processes.

Such encounters with ICTGs and other professionals revealed moments when these young people could be reached, sometimes through outreach efforts. These reachable moments allowed for better engagement and trust to be built with young people.

This raised a key question around whose interests are best served through these procedures and barriers, highlighting a tension between what was considered in the best interests – by the state or by young people themselves. Here we questioned whether years of waiting for legal status, having to tell and retell their accounts of migration and exploitation again and again, could ever be in young people's best interests.

Hearing directly from young people about what outcomes that, beyond their mere survival, they thought best for them, revealed their search for safety and the restoration of everyday life. Rights to move forward, and where possible develop in various facets of their lives, were much wanted but variably realised. Young people drew on their personal histories and original motivations for migration to find strength. They discussed their active search for safety and protection, drew on and spoke about their strengths and capabilities and how they endured the protracted and often politicised processes they found themselves in. ICTGs supported young people through these processes and systems, giving them hope about their personal future aspirations.

The views of children and young people affected by human trafficking have rarely been requested or included in the literature about them. In addition, this literature tends to focus overwhelmingly on negative outcomes and negative consequences (Hynes, 2024). We suggest that taking the participation of children and young people seriously could mean a better understanding of not only the lives of young people, but also their focus on positive outcomes in their post-trafficking lives, for the human trafficking sector in the UK. An overall lack of focus on longer-term outcomes for these young people is striking. During our two studies, young people's participation and views led to new and different perspectives around positive outcomes that are relatively unexplored.

Without these, we risk defining young people solely through their past traumatic experiences, denying their agency and ability to move forward with their lives. We suggest that the turn in the field of modern slavery towards including adult survivors in research also needs to be extended to welcome a young 'survivor turn' (Hynes, 2022), centring children and young people's participation and views.

These new and different perspectives led to the development of a much-needed Creating Stable Futures Positive Outcomes Framework (CSF-POF) for young survivors of human trafficking. Its 25 distinct 'outcomes' and 86 associated 'indicators' were grouped around the four General Principles of the UNCRC (see Table 7.1). The first ever implementation of this framework with young people – within the ICTG service – is also detailed in full, with reflections on adaptations in practice. Combined, these point us and the sector towards a much more positive discourse around children and young people affected by human trafficking in the UK as well as the possibility for creating more stable futures.

New insights and directions from child-centred research

In the UK, we have much to learn about human trafficking beyond a focus on the numbers of people referred into the National Referral Mechanism (NRM). NRM statistics do not reveal much of what is important to young people themselves. Nor do they reveal the backstories of how children and young people came to arrive into the UK, the contexts in their countries of origin, the drivers and dynamics of their migration, the journeys made, the exploitation experienced, their striving and strengths or the capabilities and agency involved (Sen, 1999). For social scientists, the inclusion of survivor views could mean inquiry into these backstories, alongside research on the histories of colonialism and imperialism and other structural and social inequalities that can lead to human trafficking.

It will be interesting to see how the inclusion of survivor views will change research on human trafficking in the future.

Highlighting different forms of exploitation at any given time influences what is considered known and, to accurately identify children and young people who have been or are at continued risk of exploitation, these forms require better understanding. If we are serious about the prevention of harm to the children and adults affected, we also need to recognise that new forms will emerge over time as our understanding grows.

Combining our two participatory research studies has resulted in three new insights, which we now outline.

The nature and descriptions of child maltreatment and exploitation shift and evolve as does the landscape of terminology connected with human trafficking, modern slavery and exploitation. This must now be changed to better reflect the realities of children's lives.

In the UK, children are now less likely to be physically abused by adults as views on what is socially acceptable have changed over time (Radford, 2011). Child protection and what constitutes child abuse or child maltreatment are thus dependent upon social norms as well as changes in legal definitions (Radford et al, 2011). Child abuse in the UK has evolved from a focus on 'battered babies' in the 1960s, to a 1990s focus on 'significant harm', and 'safeguarding and promoting the welfare of the child' in the new millennium (Parton, 2007). Firmin's 'contextual safeguarding' has brought a new lens to a child protection system that has 'resulted in children, whose lives are in danger, sitting beyond the parameters of the systems designed to protect them from harm' (2020: 250). Areas of child protection referred to here relate to adolescents, families and broader communities that past child protection systems did not reach, beyond the home environment to where 'extra-familial harms' occur (Firmin, 2020). This broadening out of safeguarding concerns to include adolescents and risks outside the home is especially relevant for young people affected by human trafficking, modern slavery and/or exploitation, yet some may also face exploitation from families and relatives.

The language describing such shifts matters, and terminology used to describe the exploitation of children has evolved over time. A clear example is the trajectory of understanding child sexual exploitation (CSE). From harmful terminology regularly referring to children as 'young prostitutes' or 'child prostitutes' responsible for 'selling sex' in the late 1980s and early 1990s, to a position in the mid-1990s where their criminalisation for behaviours resulting from abuse was increasingly challenged (Scott et al, 2019). Following years of campaigning and awareness raising to have young people responded to as 'victims' of child sexual abuse (CSA), these pejorative terms were gradually replaced by the term CSE. Beckett et al outline CSE as a form of CSA distinguished by the presence of some form of 'exchange' wherein the child or young person 'receives, or believes they will receive, something they need or want' and the perpetrator or facilitator 'gains financial advantage or enhanced status from the abuse' (2017: 8). Abuse of an unequal balance of power is the context in which such 'exchange' occurs, together with inadequate protective structures to mediate against this. Hallett charts this journey of representation from 'child prostitution' to 'child sexual exploitation' and states:

> This reconceptualisation has formed a paradigm shift in how we understand the problem and those caught up in it – moving from an issue in which young people were positioned primarily as offenders of criminal or anti-social behaviour, to one where they are now looked on as victims of abuse. (Hallett, 2017: 11)

This is not, she notes, 'simple semantics': such terminology embodies and influences how 'agency, responsibility, blame, and conceptions of vulnerability' in relation to children are interpreted in policy and practice.

Although CSE internationally sits within definitions of human trafficking, within the UK, policies and practice for CSE and human trafficking have developed separately. This

CONCLUSIONS, NEW INSIGHTS AND NEW DIRECTIONS

is changing slightly, as more UK-born children are being referred into the NRM due to CSE. Relatively new terms such as 'county lines', in place of more formal descriptors of child criminal exploitation (CCE), have also emerged. Viewing children who have been criminally exploited as perpetrators or 'victims' of a crime – and what of this might constitute child abuse – all differently situate the child.

This connects to similar transitions in terminology and related arguments on their implications for protection. As set out in Chapter 1, 'human trafficking' and 'human smuggling' are often confused and the term modern slavery itself is contested. 'Exploitation' as a term appears in the Palermo Protocol which sets out an open-ended list of examples of treatment that constitute it to allow flexibility of interpretation. In other words, key terms employed in this space are often contested, sometimes vague or inconsistent, and can be confusing and challenging for those working alongside young people as well as for young people themselves.

More broadly, the use of terms such as 'slavery', 'victim' and 'survivor' (and the binary positioning of these) can be, as recognised by Hallett, 'historically situated and conceptually loaded' (2017: 11) and have implications for the positioning of children in relation to their protection.

The reality is often more complex, contested, nuanced and interrelated, for example, Skrivankova (2010) describes a 'continuum of exploitation' between decent work and forced labour. In doing so, Skrivankova suggests the reason why there is no firm definition of 'exploitation' is that 'the real-life experiences of workers ... are rarely static' and that 'permutations of experiences' cover this broad range from optimum to the worst forms of labour (2010: 109).

Terms are powerful as they influence perception, awareness and treatment of children and young people and, in turn, practice. The contested nature of terminology used to describe human trafficking, modern slavery and exploitation is at present indicative of their politicised nature rather than being based on empirical reality. The way in which these topics get framed – as individual accounts requiring a criminal justice response that ignores wider structural forces – is problematic. Alternatively, being framed as a series of harms and risks that do not allow a focus on protective factors or positive futures is also part of this difficulty. Bureaucratic categories rarely reflect the reality of people's lives, or their heterogeneity, and people categorised in relation to modern slavery are no exception (Zetter, 2007). Such et al (2022) write about the need for a 'deep literacy' around exploitation and modern slavery, and how a lack of this can stymy efforts at prevention. Skeels and Bashir (2024) explore such literacy in relation to children and young people, drawing on examples of UK-based research on child modern slavery. For example, the lack of literacy in relation to the Modern Slavery Act 2015 (MSA 2015) and children with both diagnosed and undiagnosed special educational needs and disabilities (SEND) in the UK is startling (Franklin et al, 2024a, b).

Definitions hold power and inform responses and safeguarding thresholds. Where these are comprehensive, they can aid and enable protection; where partial, limited or their interpretation is insufficiently nuanced, the opposite can be true. A key barrier to safeguarding children and young people who have been affected by human trafficking is the way in which they themselves are perceived, and how crimes they may have committed, as part of their exploitation, are viewed.

There is a relationship between exploitation, child safeguarding and protection which calls for 'exploitation' to be more firmly recognised as a fifth form of child maltreatment, alongside physical, sexual and emotional abuse and neglect.

As in cases of child maltreatment, age and severity of abuse/exploitation can be associated with adverse outcomes. However, these consequences vary; reflecting on the interactions with the young people affected by human trafficking engaged in both our studies, and knowing that various forms of exploitation they had encountered were exploitative and abusive, led us to the realisation that, in child maltreatment terms, 'exploitation' could – or should – be more firmly recognised as abuse. This relates to all children, regardless of their ethnicity, gender, religion, language, family background, abilities or other status, including immigration status.

Over the last decade, the numbers of children and young people being referred into the NRM has risen year-on-year. The forms of exploitation experienced by children have also diversified and there is recognition that multiple forms of exploitation can occur simultaneously and be interrelated. Skeels et al (2024) and others argue that the categories of exploitation in the NRM, as well as the processes for recording these, are insufficiently nuanced to reflect either the lived experiences of children and young people affected by exploitation or what professionals supporting these children and young people are aware of and addressing through their practice. The concern here is that through such 'multiple forms of exploitation crudely categorised' (Skeels et al, 2024: 22) the realities of abuses of children and young people amid exploitation and human trafficking can be missed or misinterpreted. As Beckett (2011) wrote in relation to CSE in Northern Ireland more than a decade ago:

> The body of research evidence concludes that there needs to be a greater shift in thinking to acknowledge that adolescents, even those who appear streetwise and in control, can also be victims of abuse as a result of their social, economic and/or emotional vulnerability. (Beckett, 2011)

Throughout this book, we have highlighted how a lack of safeguarding and protection for children and young people affected by human trafficking can occur due to abuses being 'hidden' through a discourse and approach which are centred on criminal justice and immigration. In addition to this, the confusion around the use of the term modern slavery and its application to children and young people, unlike the clear and well-accepted identification of the four forms of child abuse as neglect, physical, sexual and emotional abuse of children, potentially further conceals rather than names the different forms of child exploitation and the abuses of children involved. In other words, reconceptualising child exploitation in the UK as child abuse could be more effective in protection terms, avoid ambiguities about a child's status, and clearly signal to professionals that the child in front of them is their concern.

Debates about harms outside the family home (Firmin, 2020) are as yet under-developed for young people arriving into the UK who have experienced exploitation, potentially across multiple locations beyond and then within the UK. We suggest 'exploitation' could and should be seen as a fifth form of child abuse within the UK, alongside neglect, physical, sexual and emotional abuse. It is suggested that all children might benefit from this recognition, whether they be born within or outside the UK or have lived experience of CSE, CCE, labour exploitation, domestic servitude or other known forms of exploitation, currently reported or that might emerge in the future. For non-UK-born children who may have experienced exploitation prior to or on arrival into the UK, a recognition of this as abuse could also facilitate better child protection and safeguarding. Being treated equally to other children in need of protection does not negate any space necessary to consider the capabilities, protective factors and resilience also set out within this book. There must be room for agency and for children and young people's participation in their own protection.

There is a need for better support for children during transitions to adult services and bridges need to be built to cross this current divide.

Both studies in this book considered an age range of young people that, in practice, spanned transitions from child to adult services and sought to understand these young people's views, perceptions and fears around becoming an adult. The CSF study included young people between 15 and 25 years old, to reflect care leaver entitlements up to age 21 or 25 if in higher education. The MS Outcomes study worked with a 15 to 18 age range, some of whom had already or were in the process of transitioning from the ICTG service. Both studies found that transitions between child and adult services involved loss of service provision, sometimes referred to as a 'cliff edge' or 'drop off' of child protection services at age 18. As we encountered in earlier chapters, this age of 17 and 18 means building futures dependent upon documentation and legal status. It is therefore at this point that a lack of knowledge about rights and entitlements to adult services can be felt most acutely.

This age is a time of multiple transitions in social, cognitive, emotional and physical development for young people, with specific needs during transitions to adulthood (Ozer et al, 2024). Taking risks at this stage is normal for adolescents but protective factors will vary. There is also a connection between the age of a child, child protection, policies and procedures, and – for non-UK-born children – their relation to immigration control. It is this period where young people with insecure immigration status can have considerable difficulties moving forward with their lives. Young people in both studies associated securing immigration status closely with their age, particularly when approaching the age of 18 and transitions to 'adulthood' and adult services, such as housing.

For young people with leaving care entitlements, rights associated with different age ranges are relevant here, although the terminology is often confusing and obtuse, based around a complex 13-week rule. Accommodation and support of separated and unaccompanied children are provided by local authorities under Section 20 of the Children Act 1989. The majority of separated young people who took part in these studies will be entitled to leaving care services under the Children (Leaving Care) Act 2000.[1] Terms applied to children include the following. 'Eligible children' are those aged 16 and 17 years old who have been 'looked after' for at least 13 weeks since they were aged 14 years and are still looked after. 'Relevant children' are those who are aged 16 or 17 years old, have been 'looked after' for at least 13 weeks since the age of 14, have been looked after for a period of time after their 16th birthday and have ceased to be looked after. 'Former relevant children' are 18 to 25 years old and have either been an eligible or relevant child. 'Qualifying care leavers' are young people aged 16 to 25 years who have been 'looked after' since the age of 16 for a period of less than 13 weeks since their 14th birthday. A 'former relevant child' aged between 18 and 21 years, or between 18 and 25 years if in full-time education, is eligible for entitlements as a care leaver. This includes a personal adviser, a pathway plan, assistance with education, training, employment, accommodation and living costs. A 'qualifying care leaver' is entitled to advice and assistance from children's services and help with accommodation during holidays if they are in higher education and away from home. However, in practice, children drop out of these systems and may not know they can request support up to the age of 25. Quite how young people perceive being called terms such as 'formerly relevant' is unclear.

The transitions young people make from child-centred protective services to adult services are complex and difficult to navigate. This has been recognised and responded to through service support for those affected by human trafficking via the Post-18 ICTGs pilot delivered by Barnardo's until this year. This pilot aimed to enable some young people in the service to be supported after they had reached 18, and upwards to the age of 25, where there was a clear and demonstrated need. There is some doubt as to whether this will be rolled out across the ICTG service in England and Wales. Empirical data from our combined research indicates that such transitional support is critical and this decision to not explicitly support is unwise.

The risks of young people reaching this stage being pushed to the edges of society and the risk of then experiencing situations of exploitation are great at this point. During such transitions to adulthood significant barriers to achieving positive outcomes are present, as young people find themselves without adequate support at this point, with the shield of support from child protection services being withdrawn. A 'transitional safeguarding' (Huegler, 2021) approach to reframe such binary thinking is much needed in the human trafficking space. If there is to be a serious focus and discourse on child protection and child development for children and young people affected by human trafficking going forward, joined-up systems and services are essential.

It is clear that any supportive, substantive bridge between child and adult services is absent and that children transitioning from child to adult services face ongoing challenges for their protection. This is something that requires further work and research to fully understand and address. Young people participating in both studies told us they wanted to be able to grow into being an adult with confidence and without fear, and some identified actual or anticipated challenges at transition. We now have the CSF-POF for children detailed in this book, as adapted and implemented in the ICTG service. We also have a Modern Slavery Core Outcome Set (MSCOS) for adults already developed.[2] Combining these frameworks and sets of outcomes could help to provide the much-needed bridge to stable and positive futures for children and young people affected by human trafficking.

And, finally ...

As more people are reached and recognised as having experienced a form of exploitation, human trafficking or modern slavery, more structural protections are needed. A cornerstone of international refugee law under the 1951 Convention relating to the Status of Refugees and its associated 1967 Protocol is the 'non-refoulement' (no return) of people seeking sanctuary from persecution. This means people cannot be returned or repatriated to a country where they are in fear of persecution. None of the young people involved in the two studies detailed here discussed either voluntary repatriation or what it would mean to 'reintegrate' into their countries of origin. In fact, the opposite was found.

Within international treaties on human trafficking and within the UK's 2015 Modern Slavery Act there is no such provision, meaning people can and are regularly returned to reintegration programmes in their countries of origin. As the Global Alliance Against Traffic in Women (GAATW) outlined in their landmark report on the 'collateral damage' of anti-trafficking practice, such reintegration efforts can be uncritically accepted: 'A plethora of actors on the anti-trafficking terrain do their work from the perspective of human rights including those who bundle off the trafficked and migrant women back to where they came from in the name of protection' (2007: vii). It should not be forgotten that for children and young people, approaching the age of 18 can involve such prospects. Holding onto a rights focus as young people who have lived experiences of exploitation and associated abuses reach this age is fundamental to the work of policy makers, professionals, practitioners and researchers alike, and firmer legal footings are vital.

Notes

one

[1] The GCR and GCM are non-binding but now widely accepted compacts that provide new normative frameworks on the movement of people globally, distinguishing refugees from migrants.

[2] The Protocol to Prevent, Suppress and Punish Trafficking in Persons, Especially Women and Children.

[3] The NRM involves a two-stage decision-making process as to whether an individual is a 'victim of modern slavery': (1) a 'reasonable grounds' (RG) decision based on all available general and specific information but falling short of conclusive proof, taken within 5 working days of referral if possible, and (2) a 'conclusive grounds' (CG) decision where there is sufficient information 'on the balance of all probabilities', as soon as possible after 30 days from the RG decision.

[4] Dottridge, M. (2017) *Eight Reasons Why We Shouldn't Use The Term 'Modern Slavery'*, viewed on 9 September 2024 at: https://www.opendemocracy.net/en/beyond-trafficking-and-slavery/eight-reasons-why-we-shouldn-t-use-term-modern-slavery/.

[5] We will now solely use ICTG not ICTA throughout this report to refer to these independent Guardians.

[6] Elsewhere in the UK, Scotland developed a non-statutory guardianship model in 2009 for all separated and unaccompanied children. The Human Trafficking and Exploitation (Scotland) Act 2015 provided for the introduction of statutory guardianships for unaccompanied children. The Scottish Guardianship Service was replaced by Guardianship Scotland in April 2023 as a statutory service, allowing any local authority or agency in Scotland to make referrals (Grant et al, 2023). There has been a Guardianship Service in Northern Ireland since 2018 for unaccompanied or separated children without someone with parental responsibility in the country.

[7] Viewed on 8 August 2024 at: https://whatworks-csc.org.uk/research/outcomes-framework-for-research/.

three

[1] Viewed on 9 October 2024 at: https://www.cypnow.co.uk/content/blogs/love-in-action/.

eight

[1] This Act amended the provisions of the 1989 Children Act.
[2] The Modern Slavery Core Outcome Set (MSCOS) comprises of 7 core outcomes – long-term consistent support; secure and suitable housing; safety from any trafficker or other abuser; access to medical treatment; finding purpose in life and self-actualisation; access to education; and compassionate, trauma-informed services – viewed on 28 November 2024 at: https://www.mscos.co.uk/.

References

Albright, K., Greenbaum, J., Edwards, S.A. and Tsai, C. (2020) 'Systematic review of facilitators of, barriers to, and recommendations for healthcare services for child survivors of human trafficking globally', *Child Abuse & Neglect*, 100: 104289.

Allain, J. (2018) 'Genealogies of human trafficking and slavery', *Routledge Handbook of Human Trafficking*, Routledge, pp 3–12.

Allsopp, J. and Chase, E. (2019) 'Best interests, durable solutions and belonging: policy discourses shaping the futures of unaccompanied migrant and refugee minors coming of age in Europe', *Journal of Ethnic and Migration Studies*, 45(2): 293–311.

Anderson, B. (2012) 'Where's the harm in that? Immigration enforcement, trafficking, and the protection of migrants' rights', *American Behavioral Scientist*, 56(9): 1241–57.

Anderson, B. (2013) *Us & Them? The Dangerous Politics of Immigration Control*, Oxford University Press.

Barlow, C., Kidd, A., Green, S.T. and Darby, B. (2021) 'Circles of analysis: a systemic model of child criminal exploitation', *Journal of Children's Services*, https://doi.org10.1108/JCS-04-2021-0016.

Barrow, J.F., Combes, H.A. and Rathbone, L. (2021) 'Using Q-methodology to explore what is valued from child sexual exploitation services: the importance of safety', *Journal of Child Sexual Abuse*, 30(6): 746–63.

Barter, C. (2009) 'In the name of love: partner abuse and violence in teenage relationships', *The British Journal of Social Work*, 39(2): 211–33.

Batomen Kuimi, B.L., Oppong-Nkrumah, O., Kaufman, J., Nazif-Munoz, J.I. and Nandi, A. (2018) 'Child labour and health: a systematic review', *International Journal of Public Health*, 63(5): 663–72.

Beckett, H. (2011) *'Not a World Away': The Sexual Exploitation of Children and Young People in Northern Ireland*, Barnardo's Northern Ireland.

Beckett, H., Holmes, D. and Walker, J. (2017) *Child Sexual Exploitation: Definition and Guide for Professionals*, Research in Practice/University of Bedfordshire.

Belsky, J. (1993) 'Etiology of child maltreatment', *Psychological Bulletin*, 114(3): 413–34.

Bhabha, J. (2008) *Independent Children, Inconsistent Adults*, United Nations.

Bhabha, J. (2009) 'Arendt's children: do today's migrant children have a right to have rights?', *Human Rights Quarterly*, 31(2): 410–51.

Bhabha, J. (2014) *Child Migration and Human Rights in a Global Age*, Princeton University Press.

Bhabha, J. (2016) *Children on the Move: An Urgent Human Rights and Child Protection Priority*, Harvard FXB Center for Health and Human Rights.

Bhabha, J. and Dottridge, M. (2016) *Recommended Principles to Guide Actions Concerning Children on the Move and Other Children Affected by Migration*, United Nations Action for Cooperation against Trafficking in Persons (UN-ACT).

Bhabha, J. and Dottridge, M. (2017) *Child Rights in the Global Compacts: Recommendations For Protecting, Promoting and Implementing the Human Rights of Children on the Move in the Proposed Global Compacts*, Save the Children and Initiative for Child Rights.

Bovarnick, S. (2010) 'How do you define a "trafficked child"? A discursive analysis of practioners' perceptions around child trafficking', *Youth and Policy*, 104: 80–96.

Boyden, J. and Hart, J. (2007) 'The statelessness of the world's children', *Children & Society*, 21: 237–48.

Broad, R. and Turnbull, N. (2019) 'From human trafficking to modern slavery: the development of anti-trafficking policy in the UK', *European Journal on Criminal Policy and Research*, 25(2): 119–33.

REFERENCES

Brodie, I., Spring, D., Hynes, P., Burland, P., Dew, J., Gani-Yusuf, L. et al (2018) *'Vulnerability' to Human Trafficking: A Study of Vietnam, Albania, Nigeria and the UK*, International Organization for Migration (IOM) and University of Bedfordshire.

Bronfenbrenner, U. (1979) *Ecology of Human Development*, Harvard University Press.

Brunovskis, A. and Surtees, R. (2007) *Leaving the Past Behind? When Victims of Trafficking Decline Assistance*, Fafo AIS and NEXUS Institute.

Bryant, K. and Joudo, B. (2015) *Promising Practices: What Works? A Review of Interventions to Combat Modern Day Slavery*, Walk Free Foundation.

Bryant, K. and Landman, T. (2020) 'Combatting human trafficking since Palermo: what do we know about what works?', *Journal of Human Trafficking*, 6(2): 119–40.

Bryman, A. (2012) *Social Research Methods* (4th edn), Oxford University Press.

Butler, J. (2006) *Precarious Life: The Powers of Mourning and Violence*, Verso.

Cannon, A.C., Arcara, J., Graham, L.M. and Macy, R.J. (2018) 'Trafficking and health', *Trauma, Violence and Abuse*, 19(2): 159–75.

Carling, J. (2014) *The Role of Aspirations in Migration*, Peace Research Institute Oslo (PRIO).

Carling, J. (2019) 'Research ethics and research integrity', in *MIGNEX Handbook*, Peace Research Institute Oslo (PRIO), Chapter 4.

Carling, J. and Collins, F. (2018) 'Aspiration, desire and drivers of migration', *Journal of Ethnic and Migration Studies*, 44(6): 909–26.

Carter, B. (2009) 'Tickbox for a child?', *International Journal of Nursing Studies*, 46: 858–64.

Chase, E. (2013) 'Security and subjective wellbeing: the experiences of unaccompanied young people seeking asylum in the UK', *Sociology of Health and Illness*, 35(6): 858–72.

Chase, E. (2020) 'Transitions, capabilities and wellbeing: how Afghan unaccompanied young people experience becoming "adult" in the UK and beyond', *Journal of Ethnic and Migration Studies*, 46(2): 439–56.

Chase, E. and Allsopp, J. (2021) *Youth Migration and the Politics of Wellbeing*, Bristol University Press.

Chuang, J.A. (2014) 'Exploitation creep and the unmaking of human trafficking law', *American Journal of International Law*, 108(4): 609–49.

Clayton, G., Firth, G., Sawyer, C. and Moffatt, R. (2021) *Immigration and Asylum Law* (9th edn), Oxford University Press.

Cockbain, E. and Olver, K. (2019) 'Child trafficking: characteristics, complexities and challenges', *Child Abuse & Neglect*, 95–116.

Cockbain, E., Bowers, K. and Dimitrova, G. (2018) 'Human trafficking for labour exploitation: the results of a two-phase systematic review mapping the European evidence base and synthesising key scientific research evidence', *Journal of Experimental Criminology*, 14(3): 319–60.

Dell, N.A., Maynard, B.R., Born, K.R., Wagner, E., Atkins, B. and House, W. (2019) 'Helping survivors of human trafficking', *Trauma, Violence, & Abuse*, 20(2): 183–96.

Denzin, N.K. (2017) *The Research Act*, Routledge.

Department of Health (2000) *Framework for the Assessment of Children in Need*, HMSO.

Dixon, L., Perkins, D.F., Hamilton-Giachritsis, C. and Craig, L.A. (2017) *The Wiley Handbook of What Works in Child Maltreatment*, Wiley-Blackwell.

Dottridge, M. (2017) 'Trafficked and exploited: the urgent need for coherence in international law', in P. Kotiswaran (ed) *Revisiting the Law and Governance of Trafficking, Forced Labor and Modern Slavery*, Cambridge University Press, pp 59–82.

ECPAT UK and Missing People (2019) *Still in Harm's Way: An Update Report on Trafficked and Unaccompanied Children Going Missing from Care in the UK*, ECPAT UK.

ECPAT UK And Missing People (2022) *When Harm Remains: An Update Report on Trafficked and Unaccompanied Children Going Missing from Care in the UK*, ECPAT UK.

Ellingsen, I., Storksen, I. and Stephens, P. (2010) 'Q methodology in social work research', *International Journal of Social Research Methodology*, 13(5): 396–409.

REFERENCES

Erikson, E. (1979) *Childhood and Society*, Vintage Books.

Faulkner, E. (2024) *Modern Slavery in Global Context*, Bristol University Press.

Faulkner, E.A. (2020) 'Historical evolution of the international legal responses to the trafficking of children: a critique', in J. Winterdyk and J. Jones (eds) *The Palgrave International Handbook of Human Trafficking*, Springer International Publishing, pp 79–95.

Faulkner, E.A. and Nyamutata, C. (2020) 'The decolonisation of children's rights and the colonial contours of the convention on the rights of the child', *The International Journal of Children's Rights*, 28(1): 66–88.

Feinstein, L., Aleghfeli, Y.K., Buckley, C., Gilhooly, R. and Kohli, R.K.S. (2021) 'Conceptualising and measuring levels of risk by immigration status for children in the UK', *Contemporary Social Science*, 16(5): 538–55.

Field, F., Miller, M. and Butler-Sloss, E.O. (2018) *Independent Review of the Modern Slavery Act*, HM Government.

Finch, N. (2014) *Always Migrants, Sometimes Children*, Garden Court Chambers/Coram Children's Legal Centre.

Firmin, C. (2017) *Contextual Safeguarding: An Overview of the Operational, Strategic and Conceptual Framework*, University of Bedfordshire.

Firmin, C. (2020) *Contextual Safeguarding and Child Protection*, Routledge.

Forrester, D. (2017) 'Outcomes in children's social care', *Journal of Children's Services*, 12(2–3): 144–57.

Franklin, A., Bradley, L., Greenaway, J. and Goff, S. (2024a) *Internal Trafficking and Exploitation of Children and Young People with Special Educational Needs and Disabilities (SEND) Within England and Wales: Understanding Identification and Responses to Inform Effective Policy and Practice*, Modern Slavery and Human Rights Policy and Evidence Centre.

Franklin, A., Bradley, L., Greenaway, J. and Goff, S. (2024b) *Opening Conversations: Improving the Early Identification of Children and Young People with SEND at Risk of Modern Slavery in England*, Modern Slavery and Human Rights Policy and Evidence Centre.

Gallagher, A.T. (2015a) 'Exploitation in migration: unacceptable but inevitable', *Journal of International Affairs*, 68(2): 55–74.

Gallagher, A.T. (2015b) 'Two cheers for the Trafficking Protocol', *Anti-trafficking Review*, 4: 14.

Garg, A., Panda, P., Neudecker, M. and Lee, S. (2020) 'Barriers to the access and utilization of healthcare for trafficked youth: a systematic review', *Child Abuse & Neglect*, 100: 104137.

Gearon, A. (2019) 'Child trafficking: young people's experiences of front-line services in England', *British Journal of Criminology*, 59(2): 481–500.

Global Alliance Against Traffic in Women (GAATW) (2007) *Collateral Damage: The Impact of Anti-trafficking Measures on Human Rights Around the World*, GAATW.

Graham, L.M., Macy, R.J., Eckhardt, A., Rizo, C.F. and Jordan, B.L. (2019) 'Measures for evaluating sex trafficking aftercare and support services: a systematic review and resource compilation', *Aggression and Violent Behavior*, 47: 117–36.

Grant, M., Fotopoulou, M., Hunter, S., Malloch, M., Rigby, P. and Taylor, K. (2023) *Survivor-Informed Support for Trafficked Children in Scotland*, University of Stirling.

Guedes, A., Bott, S., Garcia-Moreno, C. and Colombini, M. (2016a) *Violence Against Women and Violence Against Children – The Points of Intersection: Causes, Consequences and Solutions*, Pan American Health Organization/World Health Organization.

Guedes, A., Bott, S., Garcia-Moreno, C. and Colombini, M. (2016b) 'Bridging the gaps: a global review of intersections of violence against women and violence against children', *Global Health Action*, 9(1): 31516.

Hallett, S. (2017) 'From "child prostitution" to "child sexual exploitation": an overview', in S. Hallett (ed) *Making Sense of Child Sexual Exploitation*, Policy Press, pp 11–34.

Hanson, K. and Lundy, L. (2017) 'Does exactly what it says on the tin?', *The International Journal of Children's Rights*, 25(2): 285–306.

Hart, J. (2006) 'Saving children: what role for anthropology?', *Anthropology Today*, 22(1): 5–8.

Hart, J. (2008) 'Children's participation and international development: attending to the political', *The International Journal of Children's Rights*, 16(3): 407–18.

Hart, J. (2014) 'Children and forced migration', in E. Fiddian-Qasmiyah, G. Loescher, K. Long and N. Sigona (eds) *The Oxford Handbook of Refugee and Forced Migration Studies*, Oxford University Press, pp 383–94.

Hart, J. and Tyrer, B. (2006) 'Research with children living in situations of armed conflict: concepts, ethics and methods', *Working Paper No.30*, Refugee Studies Centre, University of Oxford.

Hart, R. (1992) *Children's Participation from Tokenism to Citizenship*, UNICEF Innocenti Research Centre.

Hek, R., Hughes, N. and Ozman, R. (2012) 'Safeguarding the needs of children and young people seeking asylum in the UK: addressing past failings and meeting future challenges', *Child Abuse Review*, 21(5): 335–48.

Hemmings, S., Jakobowitz, S., Abas, M., Bick, D., Howard, L.M., Stanley, N. et al (2016) 'Responding to the health needs of survivors of human trafficking: a systematic review', *BMC Health Services Research*, 16(1): 2–9.

Hodkinson, S.N., Lewis, H., Waite, L. and Dwyer, P. (2021) 'Fighting or fuelling forced labour? The Modern Slavery Act 2015, irregular migrants and the vulnerabilising role of the UK's hostile environment', *Critical Social Policy*, 41(1): 68–90.

Holmes, D. (2022) 'Transitional safeguarding: the case for change', *Practice*, 34(1): 7–23.

Howard, N. and Okyere, S. (2022) *International Child Protection: Towards Politics and Participation*, Springer International Publishing.

Huegler, N. (2021) *Mapping the Policy and Practice Landscape of Safeguarding Young People from Extra-Familial Risks and Harms (EFRH)*, Discussion Paper 2, University of Sussex.

Hurley, B., John-Baptiste, M. and Pande, S. (2015) *Free to Move, Invisible to Care*, ICARUS and NSPCC.

Hynes, P. (2009) 'Contemporary compulsory dispersal and the absence of space for the restoration of trust', *Journal of Refugee Studies*, 22(1): 97–121.

Hynes, P. (2010) 'Global points of "vulnerability": understanding processes of the trafficking of children and young people into, within and out of the UK', *The International Journal of Human Rights*, 14(6): 952–70.

Hynes, P. (2015) 'No "magic bullets": children, young people, trafficking and child protection in the UK', *International Migration*, 53(4): 62–76.

Hynes, P. (2022) 'Exploring the interface between asylum, human trafficking and/or "modern slavery" within a hostile environment in the UK', *Social Sciences*, 11(6): 246.

Hynes, P. (2024) 'Human trafficking and outcomes for children and young people in the UK', *Contemporary Social Science*, 19(5): 1–24.

Hynes, P. (2025) 'Evaluation of a trial of independent child trafficking advocates', in E. Cockbain, A. Sidebottom and S. Zhang (eds) *Evaluating Anti-trafficking Interventions: Critical Reflections and Lessons from the Field*, UCL Press.

Hynes, P., Connolly, H. and Duran, L. (2022) *Creating Stable Futures: Human Trafficking, Participation and Outcomes for Children*, Sheffield Hallam University, University of Bedfordshire and ECPAT UK.

Hynes, P. and Dottridge, M. (2024) 'The ethics of research into human trafficking beyond "do no harm": developing a "living" ethical protocol', in E. Faulkner (ed) *Modern Slavery in Global Context*, Bristol University Press, pp 113–44.

Hynes, P., Burland, P., Thurnham, A., Dew, J., Gani-Yusuf, L., Lenja, V. et al (2019) *'Between Two Fires': Understanding Vulnerabilities and the Support Needs of People from Albania, Vietnam and Nigeria Who Have Experienced Human Trafficking into the UK*, International Organization for Migration (IOM) and University of Bedfordshire.

Ibrahim, A., Abdalla, S.M., Jafer, M., Abdelgadir, J. and De Vries, N. (2019) 'Child labor and health: a systematic literature review of the impacts of child labor on child's health in low- and middle-income countries', *Journal of Public Health*, 41(1): 18–26.

International Labour Organization (2012) *ILO 2012 Global Estimate of Forced Labour*, International Labour Organization.

REFERENCES

Jacobsen, K. and Landau, L.B. (2003) 'The dual imperative in refugee research: some methodological and ethical considerations in social science research on forced migration', *Disasters*, 27(3): 185–206.

Jewkes, R., Willan, S., Heise, L., Washington, L., Shai, N., Kerr-Wilson, A. et al (2021) 'Elements of the design and implementation of interventions to prevent violence against women and girls associated with success: reflections from the What Works To Prevent Violence Against Women And Girls? Global Programme', *International Journal of Environmental Research and Public Health*, 18(22): 12129.

Kastberg, N. (2002) 'Strengthening the response to displaced children', *Forced Migration Review*, 15(1), 4–6.

Keeble, J., Fair, A. and Roe, S. (2018) *An Assessment of Independent Child Trafficking Advocates Interim Findings*, Research Report 101, Home Office, London.

Keeling, J. and Goosey, D. (2021) *Safeguarding Across the Life Span*, Sage Publications.

Kelly, E. and Bokhari, F. (2012a) 'Separated children in the UK: policy and legislation', in *Safeguarding Children from Abroad*, Jessica Kingsley Publishers, pp 1–176.

Kelly, E. and Bokhari, F. (2012b) 'Safeguarding children from abroad: refugee, asylum seeking and trafficked children in the UK', in *Safeguarding Children from Abroad*, Jessica Kingsley Publishers.

Kiss, L. and Zimmerman, C. (2019), 'Human trafficking and labor exploitation: toward identifying, implementing, and evaluating effective responses', *PLoS Medicine*, 16(1): e1002740.

Knight, L., Xin, Y. and Mengo, C. (2022) *A Scoping Review of Resilience in Survivors of Human Trafficking*, Sage Publications.

Kohli, R.K.S., Hynes, P., Connolly, H., Thurnham, A., Westlake, D. and D'Arcy, K. (2015) *Evaluation of Independent Child Trafficking Advocates Trial: Final Report*, Research Report 86, Home Office.

Kohli, R.K.S., Connolly, H., Stott, H., Roe, S., Prince, S., Long, J. and Gordon-Ramsay, S. (2019) *An Evaluation of Independent Child Trafficking Guardians – Early Adopter Sites: Final Report*, Research Report 111, Home Office.

La Valle, I., Hart, D., Holmes, S. and Pinto, V.S. (2019) *How Do We Know If Children's Social Care Services Make a Difference? Development of an Outcomes Framework*, Nuffield Foundation and Rees Centre, University of Oxford.

Laird, J.J., Klettke, B., Hall, K., Clancy, E. and Hallford, D. (2020) 'Demographic and psychosocial factors associated with child sexual exploitation: a systematic review and meta-analysis', *JAMA Network Open*, 3(9): e2017682.

Lebaron, G., Pliley, J.R. and Blight, D.W. (2021) *Fighting Modern Slavery and Human Trafficking*, Cambridge University Press.

Leon, L. and Rosen, R. (2023) 'Unaccompanied migrant children and indebted relations: weaponizing safeguarding', *Child & Family Social Work*, 28(4): 1056–65.

Lipsky, M. (2010) *Street Level Bureaucracy*, Russell Sage Foundation.

Lloyd, J., Manister, M. and Wroe, L. (2023) 'Social care responses to children who experience criminal exploitation and violence: the conditions for a welfare response', *British Journal of Social Work*, 53(8): 1–19.

Lott, N., Vargas-Gorena, P. and Schwarz, K. (2023) *Advancing a Child Rights Informed Approach to Antislavery Policy and Practice: A Systematic Review of Literature at the Intersection of Children's Rights and Modern Slavery*, ILO and IOM.

Lowicki, J. (2002) 'Beyond consultation: in support of more meaningful adolescent participation', *Forced Migration Review*, (15): 33–5.

Lundy, L. (2007) '"Voice" is not enough: conceptualising Article 12 of the United Nations Convention on the Rights of the Child', *British Educational Research Journal*, 33(6): 927–42.

Lundy, L. (2018) 'In defence of tokenism? Children's right to participate in collective decision-making', *Childhood*, 25(3): 340.

Lundy, L. (2025) 'Vulnerability should not eclipse agency: children's perspectives on their own lives', in T. Haugli and M. Martnes (eds) *Perspectives on Children, Rights and Vulnerability*, Scandinavian University Press, pp 31–49.

REFERENCES

Maguire, M.H. (2005) 'What if you talked to me? I could be interesting! Ethical research considerations in engaging with bilingual/multilingual child participants in human inquiry', *Forum: Qualitative Social Research*, 6(1).

Malhotra, A. and Elnakib, S. (2021) '20 years of the evidence base on what works to prevent child marriage: a systematic review', *Journal of Adolescent Health*, 68(5): 847–62.

Maternowska, M.C., Shackel, R.L., Carlson, C. and Levtov, R.G. (2021) 'The global politics of the age-gender divide in violence against women and children', *Global Public Health*, 16(3): 354–65.

Maternowska, M.C., Gould, C., Amisi, M.M. and Van Der Heyde, J. (2024) 'INSPIRE: seven strategies for ending violence against children – exploring knowledge uptake, use and impact', *Child Protection and Practice*, 1: 100008.

Meloni, F. and Humphris, R. (2021) 'Citizens of nowhere? Paradoxes of state parental responsibility for unaccompanied migrant children in the United Kingdom', *Journal of Refugee Studies*, 34(3): 3245–63.

Melrose, M. and Pearce, J. (2013) *Critical Perspectives on Child Sexual Exploitation and Related Trafficking*, Palgrave Macmillan.

Morrison, J. and Crosland, B. (2001) *The Trafficking and Smuggling of Refugees: The End Game in European Asylum Policy?* Working Paper No. 39, UNHCR.

Moynihan, M., Pitcher, C. and Saewyc, E. (2018a) 'Interventions that foster healing among sexually exploited children and adolescents: a systematic review', *Journal of Child Sexual Abuse*, 27(4): 403–23.

Moynihan, M., Mitchell, K., Pitcher, C., Havaei, F., Ferguson, M. and Saewyc, E. (2018b) 'A systematic review of the state of the literature on sexually exploited boys internationally', *Child Abuse & Neglect*, 76: 440–51.

Nash, K. (2012) 'Human rights, movements and law: on not researching legitimacy', *Sociology (Oxford)*, 46(5): 797–812.

O'Connell, C. (2024) 'The coloniality of modern slavery in Latin America', in E. Faulkner (ed) *Modern Slavery in Global Context*, Bristol University Press, pp 53–80.

O'Connell Davidson, J. (2011) 'Moving children? Child trafficking, child migration, and child rights', *Critical Social Policy*, 31(3): 454–77.

O'Connell Davidson, J. (2013) 'Telling tales: child migration and child trafficking', *Child Abuse & Neglect*, 37(12): 1069–79.

Okech, D., Choi, Y.J., Elkins, J. and Burns, A.C. (2018) 'Seventeen years of human trafficking research in social work: a review of the literature', *Journal of Evidence-Based Social Work*, 15(2): 102–21.

Ottisova, L., Hemmings, S., Howard, L.M., Zimmerman, C. and Oram, S. (2016) 'Prevalence and risk of violence and the mental, physical and sexual health problems associated with human trafficking: an updated systematic review', *Epidemiology and Psychiatric Sciences*, 25(4): 317–41.

Ozer, E.J., Abraczinskas, M., Suleiman, A.B., Kennedy, H. and Nash, A. (2024) 'Youth-led participatory action research and developmental science: intersections and innovations', *The Annual Review of Developmental Psychology*, 6: 401–23.

Parton, N. (2007) *Safeguarding Children: A Socio-historical Analysis*, Elsevier.

Parton, N. (2014) *The Politics of Child Protection: Contemporary Developments and Future Directions*, Palgrave Macmillan.

Pearce, J., Hynes, P. and Bovarnick, S. (2013) *Trafficked Young People*, Routledge.

Peters, M.D.J., Godfrey, C.M., Khalil, H., McInerney, P., Parker, D. and Soares, C.B. (2015) 'Guidance for conducting systematic scoping reviews', *International Journal of Evidence-based Healthcare*, 13(3): 141–6.

Piddington, G., MacKillop, E. and Downe, J. (2024) 'Do policy actors have different views of what constitutes evidence in policymaking?', *Policy & Politics*, 52(2): 239–58.

Pinheiro, P.S. (2006) *World Report on Violence Against Children*, United Nations.

Quijano, A. (2000) 'The coloniality of power: Eurocentrism and Latin America', *Nepantla*, 1(3): 538–80.

Radford, L. (2017) 'Child abuse and neglect: prevalence and incidence', in C. Hamilton-Giachritsis, L. Dixon, L.A. Craig and D.F. Perkins (eds) *The Wiley Handbook of What Works in Child Protection: An Evidence-Based Approach to Assessment and Intervention in Child Protection*, Wiley-Blackwell, pp 15–28.

REFERENCES

Radford, L., Allnock, D. and Hynes, P. (2015a) *Promising Programmes to Prevent and Respond to Child Sexual Abuse and Exploitation*, UNICEF.

Radford, L., Allnock, D. and Hynes, P. (2015b) *Preventing and Responding to Child Sexual Abuse and Exploitation: Evidence Review*, UNICEF.

Radford, L., Allnock, D., Hynes, P. and Shorrock, S. (2020) *Action to End Child Sexual Abuse and Exploitation: A Review of the Evidence*, UNICEF.

Radford, L., Corral, S., Bradley, C., Fisher, H., Bassett, C., Howat, N. and Collinshaw, S. (2011) *Child Abuse and Neglect in the UK Today*, NSPCC.

Ramazanoglu, C. and Holland, J. (2002) *Feminist Methodology: Challenges and Choices*, Sage Publications.

Richmond, A.H. (1994) *Global Apartheid*, Oxford University Press.

Rigby, P. (2011) 'Separated and trafficked children: the challenges for child protection professionals', *Child Abuse Review*, 20(5): 324–40.

Rigby, P. and Ishola, P. (2016) 'Child protection for child trafficking victims', in M. Malloch and P. Rigby (eds) *Human Trafficking*, Edinburgh University Press, pp 84–102.

Rigby, P., Malloch, M. and Hamilton-Smith, N. (2012) *A Report on Child Trafficking and Care Provision: Towards Better Survivor Care*, Universität Tübingen.

Robyn, R. (2004) 'Introduction: national versus supranational identity in Europe', in R. Robyn (ed) *The Changing Face of European Identity*, Routledge, pp 15–24.

Scott, S., McNeish, D., Bovarnick, S. and Pearce, J. (2019) *What Works in Responding to Child Sexual Exploitation*, University of Bedfordshire and Barnardo's.

Sen, A. (1999) *Development as Freedom*, Oxford University Press.

Setter, C. (2017) 'Unaccompanied asylum-seeking children and trafficked children', in K.S. Greene and L. Alys (eds) *Missing Persons*, Routledge, pp 64–76.

Shrimpton, H., Baker, C., MacLeod, K., Spencer, S., Ellis, N. and Scholes, A. (2024) *Independent Child Trafficking Guardian (ICTG) MSA Evaluation*, Research Report, Home Office.

Shrimpton, H., Kamvar, R., Harper, J., Gordon-Ramsay, S., Long, J. and Prince, S. (2020) *An Assessment of Independent Child Trafficking Guardians*, Research Report 120, Home Office.

Sidebottom, A., Boulton, L., Cockbain, E., Halford, E. and Phoenix, J. (2020) 'Missing children: risks, repeats and responses', *Policing & Society*, 30(10): 1157–70.

Simkhada, P., Van Teijlingen, E., Sharma, A., Bissell, P., Poobalan, A. and Wasti, S.P. (2018) 'Health consequences of sex trafficking: a systematic review', *Journal of Manmohan Memorial Institute of Health Sciences*, 4(1): 130–50.

Skeels, A. (2014) *Beyond 'Boxed In': Reconfiguring Refugee Children's Participation in Protection in Kyaka II.*, Swansea University.

Skeels, A. and Bashir, F. (2024) *Prevention of Child Trafficking and Exploitation: A Synthesis of Modern Slavery and Human Rights Policy and Evidence Centre Funded Research on Child Trafficking and Child Exploitation (2020–24)*, Report 2, Modern Slavery and Human Rights Policy and Evidence Centre.

Skeels, A., Huxley, K. and Stott, H.S. (2024) *Outcomes for Children and Young People Affected by Modern Slavery: An Analysis of Independent Child Trafficking Guardianship Service Support in England and Wales*, Modern Slavery and Human Rights Policy and Evidence Centre.

Skrivankova, K. (2010) *Between Decent Work and Forced Labour: Examining the Continuum of Exploitation*, Joseph Rowntree Foundation.

Solomos, J. (1989) *Race and Racism in Contemporary Britain*, Palgrave Macmillan.

Stalford, H. and Lundy, L. (2022) 'Children's rights and research ethics', *The International Journal of Children's Rights*, 30(4): 891–3.

Such, E., Laurent, C., Jaipaul, R. and Salway, S. (2020) 'Modern slavery and public health: a rapid evidence assessment and an emergent public health approach', *Public Health*, 180: 168–79.

Such, E., Aminu, H., Barnes, A., Hayes, K. and Ariyo, M.D. (2022) *Prevention of Adult Sexual and Labour Exploitation in the UK: What Does or Could Work?* Modern Slavery and Human Rights Policy and Evidence Centre.

REFERENCES

Sundbäck, L. (2024) 'Exploring sensemaking of trust through the lens of time: Finnish welfare professionals' perspectives on institutional encounters with forced migrants in the neoliberal welfare state', *Time & Society*, 33(4): 373–94.

Third, A., Lala, G., Collin, P., De los Reyes, P. and Hemady, C. (2020) *Child-centred Indicators for Violence Prevention: Summary Report on a Living Lab in the City of Valenzuela, Philippines*, Western Sydney University.

Thorsen, A.A. and Størksen, I. (2010) 'Ethical, methodological, and practical reflections when using Q methodology in research with young children', *Operant Subjectivity*, 33(1/2): 3–25.

Todres, J. and Kilkelly, U. (2025) *Children's Rights and Children's Development: An Integrated Approach*, NYU Press.

UNICEF (2015) *The State of the World's Children 2015: Re-imagine the Future: Innovation for Every Child*, UNICEF.

van Liempt, I. (2007) *Navigating Borders: Inside Perspectives on the Process of Human Smuggling into the Netherlands*, Amsterdam University Press.

Warrington, C. (2020) *Creating a Safe Space: Ideas for the Development of Participatory Group Work to Address Sexual Violence with Young People*, University of Bedfordshire.

Watts, S. and Stenner, P. (2012) *Doing Q Methodological Research: Theory, Method and Interpretation*, Sage Publications.

Wroe, L.E. (2021) 'Young people and "county lines": a contextual and social account', *Journal of Children's Services*, 16(1): 39–55.

Wroe, L.E. and Manister, M. (2024) 'Relationship of trust and surveillance in the first national piloting of contextual safeguarding in England and Wales', *Critical and Radical Social Work*, 12(2): 1–25.

Yuval-Davis, N., Wemyss, G. and Cassidy, K. (2019) *Bordering*, Polity.

Zetter, R. (2007) 'More labels, fewer refugees: remaking the refugee label in an era of globalization', *Journal of Refugee Studies*, 20(2): 172–92.

Zimmerman, C., McAlpine, A. and Kiss, L. (2015) *Safer Labour Migration and Community-Based Prevention of Exploitation: The State of the Evidence for Programming*, Freedom Fund/London School of Hygiene and Tropical Medicine.

Index

References to figures appear in *italic* type; those in **bold** type refer to tables. References to endnotes show both page and note numbers (231n3).

A

accommodation
  age/stage-appropriate
    benefits 75, 85–6, 89–90
  mis-assignment risks 55–6, 86
adolescence, risk factors 98–9, 149
Allsopp, J. 5, 47, 61, 80
Arendt, Hannah 6
aspirations 5, 104
'assessment triangle' 98
asylum and
  immigration procedures
  delays and opportunities
    limitations 49, 52–4, 99–100
  legal status, detrimental
    delays 63, 66–8
  structural discrimination
    46–8, 108

B

Barnardo's 18, 55, 75, 150. *see also* Independent Child Trafficking Guardianship (ICTG) service
Barrow, J.F. 137
Bashir, F. 146
Beckett, H. 144, 147
being believed 46–8, 114–199
best interests 7, 63–81, 141
  contextual safeguarding 78
  families, reunification and safe contact 77–80
  ICTGs support and trust valued 70–6, 81, 89, 141
  legal representation 68–70
  legal status, detrimental delays 63, 66–8, 80–1, 141
  protective care 76–7
  state policy inequalities 64–5
  UNCRC principle (Article 3) 64
Bhabha, J. 6–7, 92, 108
Bovarnick, S. 93
Bryant, K. 19–20

C

case-closure summaries 36–7
care 59–61
cared for 76–7
Chase, E. 5, 14, 47, 61, 80, 83
child criminal exploitation (CCE) 12, 15, 145
child development 97–9
child sexual exploitation (CSE) 12, 15, 144–5, 147
child-centred research, insights
  exploitation as abuse, recognition needed 146–8

INDEX

maltreatment/exploitation, changing terminology 143–6
survivor views, inclusion benefits 142–3
transitioning to adult services, challenges 148–51
Children (Leaving Care) Act (2000) 149–50
Children & Young People Now 60
Children Act (1989) 11, 149
Children Act (2004) 11
Clayton, G. 15, 46–7
Climbié, Victoria 11
Cockbain, E. 33
'collateral damage' 152
contextual safeguarding 12, 78, 93–4, 98, 143
contribute to society 119, 121
Creating a Stable Futures Positive Outcomes Framework (CSF-POF) 123–38, 142
  child/young people centred 4–5
  implementation in MS Outcomes study 132–8, 142
  multi-level appliances 131–2
  outcomes, identification process 125–6, *126*, 137
  outcomes and indicators **127–31**
  participation and representation 21–3, 26
  revisions ongoing 138
Creating Stable Futures: Human Trafficking, Participation and Outcomes for Children (CSF Study) 2, 31–4
  approach influences 27–30
  been listened to/understood 110–11, 113–15
  care system, expressed needs 59–61
  contribute to society 119
  ethical considerations 39–42
  family reunification 79
  GP access problems 100
  ICTGs support valued 73–4
  interpreter issues 52
  key learning points 37–9, 42–3
  legal status, importance of 66–7, 68–70
  life stability aims 102
  methods summary 31–5, **32**
  missed education 53–4, 99–100
  non-discrimination realities 46, 47–9, 53–4
  outcomes definition 20
  practice evidence and literature reviews 32–4
  professionals, good/bad encounters 55–9, 62, 118–19
  protective care 76–7
  purpose and participants 3–4, 25–6, 31, 141–2
  recognition and contribution 109
  research limitations 30–1
  safety priorities 84–5, 91, 104
  study partnership 3
  timeline 2–3
  transitioning challenges 149
  workshop objectives 124

D

Dell, N.A. 20
Dottridge, M. 6, 41

E

educational opportunities
  asylum related limitations 52–4, 66–7, 99–100
  ICTG support 54–5
  protective spaces 96
equality/inequality 48–50
Erikson, E. 97
enjoy life 103–4
Every Child Protected Against Trafficking (ECPAT UK) 3
'exploitation creep' 16

F

family 77–80
Firmin, C. 78, 93, 143
Freire, Paulo 27
friendship guidance/networks 74–5, 87, 88–9, 121

G

Global Alliance Against Traffic in Women (GAATW) 152

Global Compact for Safe, Orderly and Regular Migration (GCM) 9
Global Compact on Refugees (GCR) 9
Grant, M. 4

H

Hallett, S. 144, 145
Hanson, K. 8
Hart, J. 28–9
Hart, R., 'ladder of participation' 109, 124
health services, access to 100–1
Holmes, D 13
Howard, N. 8–9, 17
Huegler, N. 98–9
human smuggling 10–11
human trafficking
  criminalization of unaccompanied children 6–7, 11, 17
  global issue 9
  human smuggling differences 10–11
  international definition 10
  modern slavery, links debate 15–16, 145
  'outcome,' meaning inconsistencies 19–21
  regulatory gaps and risks 92–3, 151–2
  UK legislation and policy 13
Hynes, P. 13, 16, 25, 31, 142

I

identity 50–2
Illegal Migration Act (2023) 18
Independent Child Trafficking Guardianship (ICTG) service 3, 18–9, 70–6
  community integration 120–1
  friendship guidance/networks 74–5, 87, 88–9, 121
  good professionals 59, 62, 101, 104–5, 141
  MS Outcomes study 3, 21, 34–6, **35**, 132–7
  non-child centred support 18–19
  positive support and trust valued 70–6, 81, 102
  Post-18 ICTGs pilot 150
  protective care 77
  religion/culture, positive support 50–2
  supportive listening and actions 111–12
  trust building, key aims 117–19
interpreter issues 52, 136–7

J

Jacobsen, K. 30

K

key learning, ethics 39–42
key learning, participatory research 37–9
Knight, L. 107–8

L

'ladder' of child participation (Hart) 109, 114, 124
Laming, Lord 11
Landau, L.B. 30
Landman, T. 19–20
legal status and documentation
  best interest struggles 63, 66–7, 80–1
  education, missed opportunities 52–4, 66–7, 99–100
  exploitation accounts 91
  legal representation struggles 68–70
  structural discrimination 47–8, 149
Leon, L. 80
life stability and control 102–4
listened to 110–14
Lowicki, J. 40
Lundy, L. 8, 27–8, 40, 110

M

missing from care 15
modern slavery
  term, awareness of 13

INDEX

term, use contentions 2, 15–16, 145, 146, 148
Modern Slavery Act (2015) 2
  awareness source 13, 146
  implementation factors 15
  implementation impacts 17–18, 152
Modern Slavery Core Outcome Set (MSCOS) 151, 154n2

N

National Referral Mechanism (NRM)
  child referrals increase 14–15, 145, 147
  decision-making process 19, 153n3
  devolved decision-making 17
  exploitation categories insufficient 147
  safeguarding overlaps 12
  statistical focus 4, 142
Nationalities and Borders Act (2022) 18
non-discrimination, principle and practice 44–62, 140–41
  asylum/immigration procedural barriers 46–8
  documentation is key 48
  inequality/equality perceptions 48–9
  missing education opportunities 52–5
  professional services needed 59–61
  professionals, variable encounters 55–9, 140–1
  UNCRC Article 2 principles 45
  young people's experiences 44–6
non-refoulement 151–2

O

O'Connell, C. 15–16
O'Connell Davidson, J. 13, 15
Okyere, S. 8–9, 17
ontological security 83, 116
outcomes, interpretation inconsistencies 19–20
Outcomes for Children and Young People Affected by Modern Slavery (MS Outcomes study) 3, 34–7
  access to health 101
  approach influences 27–30
  been listened to/understood 111–14
  best interest decisions 68, 69
  contribute to society 119–20
  CSF-POF influenced analysis 132–3
  education as significant 54–5
  equality/inclusion perceptions 50–2
  ethical considerations 39–42
  ICTGs support and trust valued 70–6, 77, 89, 104–5, 111–12, 117–19
  interpreter issues 136–7
  key learning points 37–9, 42–3
  life stability/control aims 102–3
  methods summary 35–7, **35**, 133
  non-discrimination realities 46, 47, 49–50
  outcomes definition 21
  purpose and participants 3, 34–5, 124, 141–2
  Q-sort statements and participant reflections 133–6, 137–8
  research limitations 30–1
  safe contact with family 79–80
  safety priorities 85
  transitioning challenges 149
  understanding/navigating actions 114–15
  Young People's Advisory Group's role 133, 137–8
Ozer, E.J. 27

P

Palermo Protocol 10, 11, 92, 145
participation and agency, child/young person 106–122, 141–2
  been listened to/understood matters 110–14
  contribute to society 119–21

protection benefits 108–9, 121
research, limited inclusion 107–8
shared encounters as
  beneficial 113–14, 122
trusted and supportive
  trust 115–19
UNCRC Article 12 107
understanding/navigating
  actions 114–15
participatory research
  ethical considerations 41–2
  key attributes 123, 124–5
  Lundy model 27–8
  participation for protection
    28–30, 40
  practitioner focus groups 37
  young people-centred, key
    elements 37–9, 42
  youth experiences focus 27–8,
    35–7
Parton, N. 12, 143
Piddington, G. 137
Pinheiro, P.S. 28, 61
police encounters 58
professionals, encounters
  with 55–9
  ICTG criticisms 59
  multi-agency support
    wanted 59–61
  police insensitivity 58, 90
  psychological safety issues 90–1
  relational safety 86–7, 88–9, 116,
    118–19
  social workers, variable
    attitudes 55–8, 62
protection, child/young person 8
  abuse types and prevalence
    11–12, 16–17
  adolescence, risk factors 98–9
  'assessment triangle' 98
  child-centred policies, lack
    of 16–18, 20, 140, 146
  contextual safeguarding 93–4
  from harm 92–7
  individual conceptions/
    comparisons 94–6
  key legislation 11
  maltreatment/exploitation,
    changing terminology 143–6

non-UK arrivals, system
  tensions 13–14
own agency 97
regulatory gaps and risks 92–3,
  147–8
safeguarding overlaps 12–13
spaces, services and friends 96
transitional safeguarding
  12–13, 151
protection, international
  child-centred policies, lack
    of 17
  displacement disruptions 6–7
  gap 8
  regulatory gaps and risks 92,
    108, 151–2

Q

Q-methodology adoptions
  MS Outcomes study 35–6,
    35, 132–6
  semi-participatory 137
  translation challenges 137

R

Radford, L. 6, 12, 76, 98, 143
Refugee Convention
  (1951) 151–2
Rosen, R. 80

S

safety, search for 82–105
  fundamental priority 84–5, 104
  ontological security 83, 116
  physical safety 85–6
  psychological safety 89–92
  relational safety 86–9, 116
scoping reviews 33
Sen, A. 46, 142
Skeels, A. 17, 29, 146, 147
Skrivankova, K. 145
Solomos, J. 54
stable lives 102–3
Stalford, H. 40
State of the World's Children
  report (2015) 17
Such, E. 146

INDEX

T

terminology 139, 143–46, 150
transitional safeguarding 12–13, 151
transitions 139, 148–51
trauma-informed approaches 26, 29, 40, 140
trauma recounts, stress of 67–8
trust 70–6, 115–19
Tyrer, B. 28

U

UN Convention on the Rights of the Child (UNCRC)
aims and General Principles 7–8
Article 2 non-discrimination 7, 44–62, 140–41
Article 3 best interests 7, 63–81, 141
Article 6 life, survival and development 7, 82–105, 141
Article 12 participation 7–9, 27–8, 61, 106–22, 141–2
enforcement gaps 8–9
Eurocentrism critique 9

UN Sustainable Development Goals (SDGs) 9
unaccompanied asylum-seeking child (UASC) 14, 108, 149, 153n6
understood 114–15

V

'voice' 17, 26–31

W

Warrington, C. 29
'what works' 6, 33
What Works for Children's Social Care 20
World Report on Violence Against Children 28
Wroe, L. 78

Y

Yuval-Davis, N. 47

Z

Zimmerman, C. 98

www.ingramcontent.com/pod-product-compliance
Lightning Source LLC
Chambersburg PA
CBHW051548020426
42333CB00016B/2160